POLICY PAPERS IN

INTERNATIONAL AFFAIRS

*

NUMBER TWO

DÉTENTE AFTER BREZHNEV: THE DOMESTIC ROOTS OF SOVIET FOREIGN POLICY

ALEXANDER YANOV

INSTITUTE OF INTERNATIONAL STUDIES
UNIVERSITY OF CALIFORNIA
BERKELEY

In sponsoring the Policy Papers in International Affairs series, the Institute of International Studies reasserts its commitment to a vigorous policy debate by providing a forum for innovative approaches to important policy issues. The views expressed in each paper are those of the author only, and publication in this series does not constitute endorsement by the Institute.

Translation by Robert Kessler

International Standard Book Number 0-87725-502-4

Library of Congress Card Number 77-620014

CONTENTS

FOREWORD

Alexander Yanov was born in Odessa in April 1930. He graduated from Moscow State University in 1953, with a degree in history.[1] A year later, he began a twenty-year period as a free-lance political writer—a period that would culminate, in late 1974, in his forced emigration from the USSR. By that time he had published more than sixty articles in a variety of Moscow newspapers and journals, as well as several books and articles that have remained unpublished in the Soviet Union. The books and some of the unpublished articles focus on the history of political opposition in Russia.

Dr. Yanov's interest in Russian history, however, has always been informed by a profound concern for understanding and influencing the Soviet present. Most of his articles deal with contemporary social and political issues, and are based upon fifteen years of traveling around the country as a special correspondent, in which capacity he interviewed hundreds of Soviet citizens in all walks of life—from collective farmers to high-level Party officials. Even when he writes about nineteenth-century Russian philosophers, it is usually in the context of an ongoing debate with contemporary "neo-Slavophils." Indeed, it was Dr. Yanov's efforts to warn of the right-wing threat posed by contemporary neo-Slavophilism that helped to create a situation in which he was faced with the options of either leaving the USSR or going to prison.

Now that he is living in the West, Dr. Yanov is eager to influence the current debate about the character and future of detente. He brings with him both a wealth of first-hand knowledge of the Soviet system and a comparative historical perspective that permit him to make an unusually subtle and sophisticated argument. Yanov is far more than a journalist: he is also an historian, a sociologist, and a political scientist. In the West, he would be known as a social scientist; in the Soviet Union, as an "intelligent," in the finest sense of that term. He brings to the study of detente a *holistic* perspective—an appreciation of the complex interrelationship between

[1]In October 1970, Yanov successfully defended a dissertation on "The Slavophils and Konstantin Leont'yev" before the Department of Philosophy, Plekhanov Institute of the National Economy, Moscow. He thereby became a *kandidat nauk*—roughly equivalent to an American Ph.D.

domestic and international environments, between politics and economics, and between the actual present and the potential future.

No simple characterization will aid the reader in comprehending the message that Yanov has to offer. In fact, those who try to pigeonhole Yanov in the familiar categories will continually be subject to surprises on a careful reading of his analysis. First, Yanov is a man with *vision*—but not the idle utopian speculation of many nineteenth-century Russian intellectuals. He avoids dreaming about the millennium, and concentrates instead on devising strategies by which the Soviet regime can develop a lasting stake in detente. Second, Yanov is a *dissident*—but this label tells us little, because Yanov is in fundamental disagreement with all the major strands of Soviet dissidence—the neo-Leninist position of Roy Medvedev, the liberal-democratic ideology of Andrey Sakharov, and the religio-nationalist doctrine of Aleksandr Solzhenitsyn. Third (and what is perhaps most intriguing about him), Yanov can be termed neither *pro-* nor *anti-Soviet*. Rather, he passionately describes a contemporary reality that he considers hideous, but within which he sees positive historical forces in the place we would least expect to find them—the central Party apparatus. But before he concludes from this that Yanov envisages the potential for a Soviet Dubcek, the reader should be forewarned that Yanov foresees nothing of the kind. Fourth, Yanov is a *Jew*—but, to conclude the string of paradoxes, he was and is vehemently opposed to the Jackson Amendment for linking American trade concessions to guaranteed Jewish emigration from the USSR.

The thrust of Yanov's analysis is that detente cannot be based upon either a strategy of political ultimata or a strategy of propping up the Soviet economy through massive economic concessions. A subtle mix of economic and political demands is required. Yanov is convinced that the current American approach to detente can at best result in only a very unstable accommodation, given the precarious domestic situation in the Soviet Union. The West, he feels, must aim toward more than merely defusing tensions: it must develop strategies for defusing tensions that will simultaneously strengthen those forces within the Soviet Establishment that have a coincidence of interests in a long-term relationship of international cooperation. Yanov is not so much interested in whether detente will survive until 1984 as in whether it will be defined in such a way as to be sustained until 2004. Herein lies the combination of vision and cold realism that Yanov brings to his analysis.

Yanov is convinced that both political and economic reforms

within the USSR are prerequisites for a long-term, stable detente. Economic reforms, based upon the generation of domestic sources of technological innovation, are necessary to create a healthy economy. Continuation of the present pattern of precarious economic performance, he argues, only strengthens the hands of those who would be likely to lead a "right-wing," nationalistic reaction against both detente and domestic disorder. However, these same forces (local Party secretaries, the "military-industrial complex," and others) are powerful enough to prevent an economic reform that would diminish their functions, prerogatives, and privileged status in the system. Hence, economic reform is impossible without a political coalition in the Central Committee among the forces which have an interest in both detente and economic reform. These forces, Yanov argues, include both a stratum of dynamic and skilled managers who, along with their "technostructure," seek a major reform of the economy and a vast stratum of central officials (of whom Brezhnev is representative) who need detente and a healthy economy in order to further their own primary goals: security from mass disorder and guarantees of their privileged access to Western travel and luxury items. Yanov wants the West to adopt policies that would facilitate a pragmatic alliance between the "aristocratizing elite" and the "technostructure" in order to break the power of entrenched interests in the USSR.

The traditional images of Soviet political structure that Westerners bring to their analyses of detente crumble in Yanov's hands. The "new class" is divided not between "scientists" and "apparatchiki," but rather between cosmopolitan central officials and parochial local officials. The managerial class is divided not only between conservatives and risk-takers, but also between managers of defense-oriented industries, who have priority access to supplies, and managers of other industries, who must live in constant uncertainty about supply availability. The burden of Yanov's first two chapters is to describe the cosmopolitan central officials and the risk-taking managers in non-defense industries, and to analyze their coincidence of interests in economic reform and detente. In the third chapter, he describes the powerful political, social, and ideological forces arrayed *against* interdependence and interpenetration with the West. Once again, Yanov's account forces us to reconsider our stereotypes. The right wing, he contends, would not be expansionist and confrontational vis-à-vis the West; rather, it would opt for a strategy of imperial isolation (a "new Byzantine Empire"), geared toward restoring order and discipline to the Soviet "bloc." In this chapter he diverges somewhat from the contemporary thrust of the earlier chapters by documenting the deep roots in Russian and Soviet history of the ideological and political foundations of a right-wing reaction.

Thus Yanov is both frightened and hopeful. He sees the current situation in the Soviet Union as transitional—inherently unstable because of the intimate relationship between political power, economic reform, and foreign policy. This leads him, in the final chapter, into the realm of policy prescription. Yanov believes that, given the current standoff in Moscow, the policies of the West may well be decisive in shaping the character of the Soviet regime after Brezhnev. Political confrontation will strengthen the forces of the right, but a policy of total appeasement will ultimately be self-defeating.

Westerners may disagree with specific points of evidence or interpretation in Yanov's analysis, but they will be hard-pressed to deny the plausibility of its thrust. Moreover, they may at points be put off by the emotional language (especially in light of the more dispassionate tone adopted in studies of the Soviet Union in recent years), but they will be the losers if they let this blind them to the reality being described.

George W. Breslauer

Berkeley, California
March 1977

Chapter I

A SKETCH OF THE SOVIET ARISTOCRACY, OR PLAYING THE DEVIL'S ADVOCATE

A. A *NEW* "NEW CLASS"?

The existence of a Soviet "new class" has been known at least since the 1930's and Trotsky's writings exposing the "bureaucratic degeneration" of the dictatorship of the proletariat. And it has been twenty years since the *term* "new class" was coined by Milovan Djilas. The way of life and customs of this "new class" have already given rise to a sea of legends and an ocean of anecdotes—a whole folklore.[1] There is nothing I can add, except my personal impressions from a visit to the home of a high Soviet official—not of the highest rank, like Brezhnev, Shelest, or Solomentsev, but one of the top "thousand" who rule the USSR today.

The house is located in a fashionable, wooded suburb and reminds one of the countryseat of a landed gentleman of medium rank. When you enter the first, enormous and bright room, you find yourself . . . in the eighteenth century. Originals by old masters hang on the walls. One has to avert one's eyes from the sparkling parquet, illuminated by a magnificent crystal chandelier. The furniture is a collection of wondrous antiques. It is a museum curator's dream. The rows of armchairs along the walls make one feel that they should be covered with plastic with a sign attached that says "Please do not touch." The hall seems to have been made ready for the kind of ball given by the nobles of Elizabeth's reign.

In your amazement you have not managed to catch your breath when a heavy, carved door opens and you are led . . . not into the next room, but into the twenty-first century. It is not a room; essentially it is a set for shooting a spectacular science fiction film. Brightly colored lampshades hang at various heights above an unfathomably deep soft carpet; the products of abstract artists' uncanny fantasies stare at you from the walls; and something made of leather,

[1] See, for example, Hedrick Smith's *The Russians* (New York: Quadrangle/The New York Times Book Co., 1976).

akin to what was known as an armchair, sits in front of an enormous color television set that picks up foreign programs.

Then you descend a narrow little varnished staircase, but of course not into the basement; this time you enter . . . the Middle Ages. Here the walls are made of rough, unfinished stones and decorated with ancient hunting weapons. The furniture and the floor are covered with the skins of wild animals, and some thick, twisted logs—probably hoary with age—smolder in the tremendous fireplace. The solemn, somber chorales of Bach wash over you from an unknown source.

The door out of the Middle Ages leads to an ordinary modern and comfortable living room, where ordinary Czech crystal gleams on glass shelves, but the batteries of Napoleon French cognac arrayed at the bar make it appear that the host, in conjunction with his high-level state functions, earns something on the side by selling liquor. In addition, there is what looks like an ordinary small white transistor radio, but you simply turn a little switch and suddenly you hear the clear and powerful voice of Radio Liberty, as if the ubiquitous "jammers" did not exist at all.

Finally, the host's study. Over the desk hangs a huge portrait of Lenin, who they say was "as simple as the truth." The bookshelves are endless. Here your amazement becomes so great that you cease to be surprised at anything. The works of Aleksandr Isayevich Solzhenitsyn peacefully coexist with the works of the "leader of the world proletariat," object of his hatred.[2]

I have seen a great deal since then. I have been the guest of well-to-do American colleagues and have even attended a reception given by a Texas lady millionaire. But in comparison with the owner of that astonishing house, all of them—including the lady millionaire—are proletarians who have nothing to lose but their chains!

The point of the picture with which I have ventured to begin my sketch is that the high Soviet official *has something to lose.* Therefore, all his actions in life and in politics are subordinated to the perfectly natural desire to consolidate his privileges. This is a fundamental fact of present-day Soviet reality, one that is well-known. It is less well-known that the "thousand" I have referred to are only the tip of the Soviet "aristocratic" iceberg. Underneath, forming the social base of this iceberg—its basic "submerged" foundation—are the broad and constantly expanding strata of the middle and lower

[2]Another such bibliophile and eager recipient of foreign information as our host, if he were an "ordinary Soviet person," could expect at least five years in a strict-regime camp.

nobility. I do not mean Party functionaries: that elite stratum, which is commonly termed the "new class," arose in the USSR back in the 1930's.[3] I am talking about the broad strata of the population that in the post-Stalin era have acquired a monopoly on travel to the West, so that they enjoy all the advantages of the Western way of life without experiencing any of its shortcomings. It was possible for these strata to appear only when the USSR became a "semi-open" system, and when commercial, scientific, cultural, and technical contacts with the West began to expand rapidly. The tens of thousands of people who provide the services required by these contacts unexpectedly obtained the exceptional privilege of living by Western standards in a country of semi-Asiatic poverty. Included in this category are the ever-growing numbers that have been designated to provide services for foreigners visiting the USSR—from drivers and shoemakers to interpreters and scientists. It also encompasses the thousands of sailors of the gigantic Soviet merchant fleet, the airline crews who maintain regular links with the West, the numerous office employees of the various Soviet missions in foreign capitals and international organizations, the scientists who work at foreign universities through "exchange" programs, the engineers who "familiarize themselves with foreign technological experience" on the spot, the journalists who deal with international affairs, the performers who present Soviet art to the world, and . . . . But it is time to make an end to this list, which threatens to use up all the remaining space granted me by my publisher.

I simply want to observe that these people constitute a large social stratum—a stratum that could be called the *new* "new class." All these people have relatives, both close and distant. It is for them that, in addition to the traditional Stalinist network of elite "distribution centers" to which "unauthorized persons are not admitted,"

[3]Here it is interesting to note the radical change in the form of the privileges of the Stalinist and post-Stalin elites—from food rations and "quitrent in kind" from the collective farms under their authority to additional pay in cash. (Of course this means only a change in the proportions of payments "in kind" to payments in cash—not a substitution of one form for the other.) In this connection, Dr. A. Katsenelinboygen has called attention to the fact that offering privileges "in kind" makes the elite far more controllable. This is because one cannot be given enough fresh eggs, choice veal, or even black caviar to last a lifetime, while cash is still cash even after a functionary loses his official position. It is not surprising that Khrushchev's son-in-law, Aleksey Adzhubey, who lost all his posts, nonetheless has "capital" to invest in parcels of land, for example, which he has purchased at suburban collective farms (according to common acquaintances in Moscow).

the network of Beryozka stores has been opened in the very heart of the country—the so-called certificate and foreign exchange stores, where it is possible to acquire goods unavailable to the population without having to go abroad. It is to give their privileges substance that there exists a huge network of second-hand stores through which surplus foreign booty is sold legally. Who has calculated how many millions of people in the USSR now make their living thanks to the fact that the Ministry of Foreign Trade has shared with them, de facto, the monopoly that was unalterable under Stalin? These are real privileges. People value them; people will fight for them. Only a new Stalin would be capable of abolishing them—with the aid of new terror on a mass scale.

Is the "new class" today the same phenomenon to which Djilas's famous book was devoted? Is it, as before, a comparatively narrow elite of functionaries who rule the country with the aid of the GULAG Archipelago and total ideological control? In that case, what could it base itself on today, now that the great GULAG has been dismantled and total ideological control lost? Have we perhaps simply failed to notice the moment when terror and control were replaced by the mass social base on which the Soviet political universe now rests? Have we failed to notice the moment when the structure of the "new class" became more complex and differentiated, when the narrow caste of the Party boyars and bureaucratic heirarchy were supplemented and, so to speak, propped up from below by a large social stratum that is surprisingly reminiscent of the traditional Russian service nobility? Indeed, the minor trade union clerk who accompanies tourist groups abroad values his privilege of bringing back Chanel No. 5 no less than the son of Politburo member Kirill Mazurov values the privilege of hunting elephants in Africa. An ordinary sailor values the privilege of exchanging his certificates for muskrat fur caps at the Murmansk or Odessa Beryozka store no less than a big boss values the privilege of importing a long black Packard.

The scale of privileges varies, but their essence is the same. Without Detente someone will lose his Chanel and muskrat fur and someone else will lose his hunting trip and Packard. Both of them will lose something they can no longer get along without. Both of them are "hooked" on Western living standards. That is why both of them are in favor of Detente; that is why both of them are Western-oriented. That is why roles within the "new class," which has grown more complex and hundreds of times larger, have been unexpectedly switched: the Western-oriented group at the very top, in the Politburo (the Centrist group), has become the political representative of a large, privileged, and Western-oriented stratum below that runs through the entire social hierarchy of Soviet society—from the middle-ranking conformist scholar who for the first time has gained the opportunity to openly acquire antiques and original works by the French Impressionists to the hairdresser who wins prizes at a competition in Brussels.

Of course, both the political aristocracy and the social aristocracy relate to the West as consumers. In general, a lumpen-parasitic psychology is characteristic of both. Those "at the top" would like to vitalize the agonizing process of communist construction by means of the stimulating achievements of bourgeois scientific and technical thought; those "below" would like to protect themselves from the semi-Asiatic poverty of the long-suffering people by means of the achievements of bourgeois consumer society.

But in both cases Detente is a prerequisite for implementing their strategies of life. It is precisely on the basis of this coincidence of interests that the sociopolitical category of the "aristocracy" has taken shape within the Soviet "elite" in the post-Stalin era.[4]

B. ELITE AND ARISTOCRACY

What is, properly speaking, an "aristocracy"? How is it different from an "elite"? The difference is that an elite is generally unstable, as it was for millennia in China, or in Byzantium, or in Soviet Russia under Stalin; that its position lacks elementary guarantees; that its members are not able to assure themselves the enjoyment of their privileges even for life, not to mention the greater concern of transmitting their privileges through inheritance. An elite depends entirely on a tyrant, no matter what he may be called—autocrat, emperor, sultan, general secretary of the party, or chairman of a people's republic.

History knows no states without elites: there are only those with stable elites and those with unstable elites. Unstable elites are the hallmark of Eastern despotism; stable, "aristocratic" elites are characteristic of European absolutism. From this standpoint, the entire history of the Russian elite is the history of its struggle for

[4]In my opinion, it is clearly wrong to equate the concepts of "elite" and "aristocracy" when speaking of present-day Soviet society. The elite (the "new class") is a far more complex and general category, encompassing several groups that have opposite and even mutually exclusive interests and contend with one another. The "aristocracy" (the *new* "new class") is only a segment of the post-Stalin elite, and not the strongest segment politically.

aristocratization—a struggle that has met with varying success, a struggle in which periods of total instability have alternated with periods of temporary stabilization. There has not been a completely stable, unqualifiedly aristocratic elite in Russia since the mid-sixteenth century. The European-type state that came into being in the revolutionary surge of liberation from the Tatars in the mid-fifteenth century made possible ideological pluralism and a stable aristocratic elite for only a brief historical interval, for one "Absolutist Century."

To this day, however, this remote historical "hinterland" of the Russian political tradition nourishes both the liberal and the elitist-aristocratic tendencies in Russian (including Soviet) life. It is why Russia has never been an Eastern despotism: no Russian tyrant has been able to make the elite completely unstable any longer than his own lifetime. After his death a struggle for the aristocratization of the elite has begun immediately (along with a struggle to liberalize the country). That is what happened after Ivan the Terrible, after Peter, after Paul, and after Nicholas I; that is what has happened since Stalin's death. It is part of the Russian historical tradition.

But at least since the mid-sixteenth century, Russia has not been a European country either. In the West both tendencies—the liberal and the aristocratic—have supplemented each other more or less harmoniously. In Russia, everything has been just the opposite: the tendency favoring liberalization has always been in mortal combat with the tendency favoring aristocratization. The outcome of this struggle has always been the accession of a new tyrant to the throne, a tyrant who has mercilessly destroyed both the liberals and the aristocrats in equal measure. And are not these two tendencies running counter to one another in precisely the same way in Russia today? Are they not leading events toward the traditional fatal outcome once again?[5]

[5]In the West, privileges have always served as the historical foundation, starting point, and prerequisite for civil rights. In Russia, privileges are regarded as the opposite pole, the absolute antipode of these rights. The West achieved its rights *through* privileges; the Russian liberals want to achieve them by *destroying* privileges. But after all, the process of incorporating guarantees into the legal standards applied to the people, the process of restricting the arbitrariness of authority, requires powerful political protection. Consummating this process by means of external pressure is inconceivable. Only internal forces that have a natural interest in consolidating their guarantees and their privileges can actually restrict authority, thereby initiating a general process of imposing restrictions on it. This is why the Soviet elite's striving for aristocratization, paradoxical as it may sound to the Western and especially to the Russian ear, may become the first step toward the liberalization of the country.

But that is another subject. Right now it is important for us to answer the question "What is the position of the Soviet aristocracy as seen through its own eyes?"

C. CHANNELS OF ARISTOCRATIZATION

First we shall attempt to prove that an aristocracy exists in the Soviet system as a social group and as a historically positive segment of the Soviet elite.

It is obvious that, in any society, people who have privileges try to consolidate them, make them stable, and promote them to the point where it becomes possible to pass them on through inheritance. In addition, I simply know this is true of Soviet society. I know it in the same way that all Soviet people know it. They know it from living—from contacts, from conversations, from the air that they breathe. Therefore, when my Western colleagues adopt a serious mien and demand that I present proof of my assertion that there are inherited privileges in the Soviet system, I cannot refrain from smiling, even though I realize that their demand is a just one. Is it not proof that everyone in Russia knows it? Is it not proof that it long ago became a banal assumption of everyday consciousness? Can there be any better proof of the existence of such intimate processes within an elite—processes that are beyond the reach of any objective means of gathering information? What means can be used to penetrate beneath the surface to the inner workings of the elite in an authoritarian society? To a Soviet person this long ago ceased to be a matter of *proof* and is rather a matter of *interpretation* of a universally known fact. Take the very simple step of surveying recent Soviet emigres (who already number more than 100,000), and you will see that they *all* know about the Soviet elite—if not in their heads, then (so to speak) in their guts.

We shall attempt to make this subjective knowledge objective. The subterranean struggle for the aristocratization of the elite must—and does—produce eruptions that reach the surface. Let us review some illustrations of this process in the Soviet political dynamic.

1. One illustration is Khrushchev's introduction of the category "politically dead" into Soviet reality. In plain language, this means that a Soviet functionary who has made an official blunder or expressed an independent opinion is no longer pronounced an "enemy of the people" and does not run the risk of getting a bullet in the back of his head or rotting in the quarries of Magadan, as was the case in Stalin's time; he will simply lose his political position. He dies

politically but remains alive physically—often with a personal pension or an office devoid of political significance. For the West this development has been a matter of little consequence. For Russian reality it is a very basic change because it fundamentally alters the atmosphere of public life, introducing the possibility of domestic political struggle instead of crude battling for physical survival. So long as they do not openly challenge authority, people in Russia have gained the right to die in their beds. No matter how paradoxical this may sound to a citizen of a law-governed state, it is the greatest gain of the post-Stalin era. At the same time it is genuine proof—it is, if you will, a kind of graphic demonstration by historical experiment—that a transition from elite *privileges* to people's *rights* (at least de facto) is possible. Indeed, the introduction of the category "politically dead" at first had significance only for the elite, only for people directly involved in politics. When the Soviet leaders introduced it, they were thinking only of their own skins, but maintaining this privilege without simultaneously granting the people certain de facto guarantees proved to be impossible.

The category "politically dead" has always been established in Russia during eras following tyrants, as was the case under Michael Fyodorovich in the seventeenth century, under Elizabeth Petrovna in the eighteenth century, and under Alexander I in the nineteenth century. It has served as the objective basis and starting point for the process of the aristocratization of the elite. Moreover, the Brezhnev regime—and this is proof that the process is *developing*—has made the position of the "nomenklatura" far more stable than it was under Khrushchev, with his frequent ministerial changes and continual reforms. Comparative statistics regarding the stability of Central Committee or Politburo members, province Party committee apparatchiki, ministry staffs, and even enterprise and institute directors will clearly demonstrate this. The objective soil in which an aristocracy can spring up has been provided.

2. This greater stability relates directly to a second indicator of the process involved in the Soviet political dynamic: a decline in the very high political mobility characteristic of the Stalin era and a severe narrowing of the channels for "moving up." In other words, an ossification of the elite typical of an era of aristocratization is taking place, and the elite is more and more openly turning into a caste. The slogan "The last shall become the first," which generally accorded with reality in the 1920's and 1930's, seems a hopeless anachronism in the Soviet Union today. Is this not indicated, for example, in the rise in the average age of the top-level staff cadre to

60-70 years in comparison with the average of 30-40 years in Stalin's time? Is it not indicated by the fact that new restrictions have been introduced into the process of selecting leading cadres?

One evidence of these new restrictions is the strict limitation on the number of members of the intelligentsia accepted into the Party since the late 1960's, as well as the sharp drop in the number of children of the intelligentsia accepted by the universities. In both cases, preference has been given to workers or their children. In essence, the open social and political discrimination characteristic of the early Soviet period has been revived. Why?

At first glance, this phenomenon might be interpreted as reflecting continuing concern on the part of the Party for maintaining at least the appearance of worker-peasant affiliation, or as indicating fear of the intelligentsia after the events of the late 1960's in Czechoslovakia. But if one considers this from the standpoint of the political dynamics within the Soviet elite, the interpretation may be much more complicated. However, this relates to a third process involved in the Soviet political dynamic—what I call "the migration to academe."

3. By "the migration to academe" I mean the acquisition of academic degrees on a massive scale by Party and state functionaries who make use of their official positions to have trained specialists subordinate to them write their candidate's and doctoral dissertations. If one undertakes to study the educational qualifications of the Soviet "nomenklatura," one is inevitably struck by the unprecedented increase in the number of functionaries who have academic degrees. Today it is considered unseemly if, for example, the vice-chairman of a city Soviet executive committee, or a provincial Party committee secretary (but not the first secretary), or a Central Committee instructor is not a candidate of sciences. The Central Committee's departmental consultants and department heads are now often doctors of sciences or academicians.

But what is the objective basis of this migration to academe? It is certainly not that these functionaries have suddenly felt an irresistible passion for knowledge: academic titles have not yet kept anyone from maintaining his ignorance in all its purity. But in the USSR these titles confer the only status that offers guarantees of lifetime privileges.

The cases of Shafarevich, Sakharov, and Levich—academicians who are in open opposition to authority and have still not been deprived of their privileges as academicians—are striking evidence of the fact that these privileges are not a dead letter but a living political reality. How is one to interpret this astonishing situation? Of course, one can assume that the academic community in the USSR is afraid of a dangerous precedent, but by itself this community is a political cipher, and it would unquestionably yield to pressure from the all-powerful Central Committee. Since the Central Committee is capable of exerting such pressure and nevertheless does not do so, what does this mean? Is the answer not obvious? Is it not that the Central Committee does not want to exert this pressure? This does not seem so paradoxical when one recalls that the Central Committee's Science Department and International Department are both headed by academicians, and that the person who might be called the manager of Detente in the USSR (I refer to the Chairman of the Committee on Scientific and Technical Ties with Foreign Countries) is also an academician, as is his vice-chairman, Kosygin's son-in-law. It is not the fate of Sakharov or Shafarevich that concerns these people, but rather their own. Let us recall that Khrushchev's son-in-law, who seemed to be all-powerful in the early 1960's, was relieved of all his positions and privileges immediately after the fall of his father-in-law, and then let us compare his fate with that of the son of former Politburo member Pyotr Shelest. Shelest proved to be more astute than Khrushchev: shortly before he fell from power, he made his son an academician—not, like Adzhubey, the editor of *Izvestiya*—for as experience has shown, even extremely high political status in the USSR guarantees nothing. In other words, he made his son practically invulnerable after his own fall from power. Does this not testify not only to the power of academic privilege, but also to the fact that the Soviet aristocrats—especially since the fall of Khrushchev—have begun to realize clearly the existence of this power?

It is interesting to note that the material perquisites of academic privilege—salaries which are enormous by Soviet standards and, what is most important, guaranteed for life—were created (or rather restored) by Stalin right after World War II, when the lagging of Soviet science, especially in the field of atomic weapons, had become a matter of life and death for the USSR. But it is important to bear in mind that under conditions in which the category "politically dead" did not exist, no status and no material position could guarantee even physical safety; therefore the academician's perquisites could not become *real* privilege under Stalin. Only in conjunction with the category "politically dead" could these perquisites be transformed into a social status and a social position invulnerable to arbitrary actions, into privilege as such. Part of the Soviet elite instinctively sensed the promise of this channel of aristocratization in an egalitarian society, and they streamed into it. This is what "the migration to academe" refers to.

Now it is possible to see the connection between "the migration to academe" phenomenon and the recent limitation on acceptance of the intelligentsia as Party members, which we discussed earlier. From this standpoint the limitation on Party membership takes on an entirely different meaning; it is a sign of an open competitive struggle to monopolize privileges and to maintain the exclusiveness of the elite caste. In the Party, workers are preferable to intelligentsia not only because they are pliable material for manipulation, but also because they will never become competitors in the academic sphere. A similar rationale underlies the limited acceptance of children of the intelligentsia by the universities. An attempt is being made to change the very makeup of the intelligentsia so as to render it intellectually lifeless—an attempt to render harmless a potential competitor without resorting to double-edged mass terror.

Let us summarize. If the leading stratum is persistently striving to gain control of the only stable status in an unstable system—and not only to gain control, but also to monopolize that status—how can one describe this process if not as an attempt to achieve the aristocratization of the elite, as an attempt to turn temporary official privileges into lifetime privileges?

4. The next process involved in the political dynamic within the Soviet elite is the attempt to find ways of making lifetime privileges hereditary. One evidence for this is an ever more obvious interest of the "nomenklatura" in property in the most bourgeois, so to speak, sense of the word. Consider their interest in land, for example—i.e., the acquisition of dachas and country homes with large lots of land as so-called "personal property." Consider also their interest in the acquisition of precious stones, gold, objets d'art, all sorts of rarities, crystal, furniture fit for museums, and so on.

If one's official position is unstable, if money is unstable, and if academic status cannot be passed on through inheritance, then what is left? The "personal property" that we are talking about. This process of acquiring personal property still awaits research, which will have to deal with what I call the "duplication phenomenon." What this refers to is that under Stalin all material privileges were departmental—i.e., depended entirely on one's official position—whereas now members of the elite who may possess, for example, departmental dachas prefer to *duplicate* them by acquiring their own. In general terms, they are using their official status to acquire things that can be passed on through inheritance.

5. A second aspect of this process of making privileges hereditary is more obvious. While academic status cannot be passed on through inheritance, it is possible to provide one's heirs with an exclusive right to such status. This is the basis for the essentially "closed" system of colleges that has taken shape during the past decade—private academies for the youth of the aristocracy. One stream of young people flows into the institutes connected with the military-industrial complex, which in an authoritarian and militarist society is privilege "worth its weight in gold." The model for these colleges is the Physicotechnical Institute, or the analogous faculties at Moscow and Leningrad universities. A second, larger stream flows into the institutes associated with contacts with foreign countries. The aristocratic families wish to keep these contacts in the hands of their children, to make them a kind of family privilege of the new aristocracy. Therefore the Institute of International Relations (MIMO), for example, or the Institute of Foreign Trade, or the faculties of journalism (especially the departments related to international affairs) are becoming closed aristocratic educational institutions. Intra-elite marriages—an even more radical means of aristocratization—have now become widespread. For example, the children of officials in the Ministry of Foreign Affairs or Foreign Trade marry only among themselves, thereby creating a living barrier to the introduction of "alien" elements into the elite.

In general, little or no importance has been attached up to now to the fact that two political-economic processes that are improper from the standpoint of law, official ideology, and semi-official morality are unfolding simultaneously in the USSR. The first is well known to the entire world: it is the process of development of economic dissidence (if one can describe it in those terms)—an underground economy that combats the state's economic monopoly—as well as political dissidence, which combats the state's monopoly on ideas. Both manifestations of this dissidence are savagely persecuted by the police agencies, the OBKhSS [Department for Combatting Embezzlement of State Property and Speculation], and the KGB [Committee on State Security], and scandals related to these persecutions agitate the Western press from time to time. Both manifestations have their prophets and interpreters in the West.

Why not make an attempt to offer a political interpretation of the second "illegal" process that has unfolded in the USSR during the post-Khrushchev period—the formation of a privileged caste in a "state that belongs to all the people"? There can be no doubt whatsoever that this caste is a "criminal" phenomenon in an egalitarian, "socialist" society—criminal from the standpoint of law, ideology, and morality, as any specialist will tell you. From the "closed" stores to the "closed" colleges, from the "closed" beaches to the "closed" film showings—all this is criminal in the USSR. Nevertheless, while the first of these "illegal" processes is openly persecuted, the second is under the protection of the authorities, who regard the very mention of "privileges" as slander against the Soviet state and social system.

Does this not mean that in the USSR there already exists a dual legality, a dual ideology, a dual morality? Does this not mean, in other words, that the process of formation of the new "new class"—which if we wish to be precise in our terminology should be referred to as the process of aristocratization of the Soviet elite—is destroying the regime's ideological foundation in the eyes of the people?

D. WHAT PREVENTS THE INSTITUTIONALIZATION OF THE ARISTOCRACY?

Despite the intensive development of the process of aristocratization of the elite, one must not lose sight of its weaknesses and its fear of publicity—i.e., its inability to surface in society as a legal phenomenon. I can see five main obstacles blocking this process—five major contradictions in the position of the emerging Soviet aristocracy.

1. First, there is the contradiction between the aristocracy and the "people," whom the aristocracy has proven incapable of feeding with black bread while consuming black caviar itself. As has been characteristic of parvenus in all ages, this aristocracy despises the people; but it also fears them. It fears what Pushkin long ago called the "mad and merciless Russian uprising"; it fears the people's traditional attachment to a "master," to a strong tsar as protection from oppression by the elite. The aristocracy knows that historically the Russian people have been able to tolerate aristocratic privilege only when such privilege has been countervailed and balanced by a strong authority at the top. In this sense the task confronting the new aristocracy is a complex one. In essence, the aristocracy has to create a new sociocultural balance of forces—i.e., it has to pay the people for its privileges in a fundamentally different way: by feeding and clothing them, putting an end to their age-old poverty, and providing them—for the first time in centuries—with at least a minimum European standard of living. The Roman emperors knew long ago that more than "circuses" are needed in order to keep the people

quiet in an autocratic country: "bread" is needed too.

2. The second contradiction in the position of the aristocracy is political. There will be no "bread" without a general reconstruction of the economy—i.e., without a political alliance with the managerial class—but even that will not be enough. The Soviet aristocracy will have to aid in the creation of a powerful social *counterculture*: a new managerial elite of the Japanese type with whom political power will have to be shared. On the other hand, the aristocracy currently shares power with the most benighted, "Black Hundred," double-dyed reactionary elements of the elite—the "rightists," who threaten the aristocracy's very existence. Why not share power with the "leftists," who will help the aristocracy consolidate its privileges? The concrete political strategy that might be adopted to resolve this contradiction in the Soviet aristocracy's position is, I repeat, incredibly complex. At this point I will say only that means of resolving it exist in principle.

3. The third contradiction is related to the aristocracy's archaic ideology, which is permeated with an egalitarian spirit and premised on the mythical "dictatorship of the proletariat." From the standpoint of this dogma, the Soviet aristocrats not only do not exist, but they *cannot* exist in a Marxist state. They are an apparition, a phantom, a product of the dissidents' sick imagination. The paradox lies in the fact that the elite, having lost its old ideological foundation and still without a new one, *is* a phantom in a certain sense. It is faced with the problem of effecting a fundamental revision of the old dogma while remaining within its framework. Stalin managed to accomplish this when he needed to do away with the "Party salary maximum" and create his own oprichnik "nomenklatura"; what is more, he cynically pronounced all the advocates of the archaic "Leninist norms" of Party life opponents of Leninism. Mao and Tito also managed to revise the dogma; Berlinguer and Marchais are managing to do so now; Dubcek and Šik managed to do it; even the Medvedev brothers are managing to do it. Why then is it impossible to revise this "elastic" doctrine for the 1001st time—to suit the purposes of the emerging aristocracy?

Of course the Party scholastics, whose thinking has been rendered hopelessly sterile by Stalin's terror and the subsequent bewildering zigzags of the "general line of the Party," are incapable of accomplishing this task. To accomplish it the aristocracy must ally itself with the most brilliant Russian intellectuals, who are concentrated today in the dissident movement—just as it must ally itself with the managers in order to resolve the first contradiction. But as is well known, due to their gross ignorance and failure to understand their own interests, the aristocrats are letting the dissidents rot in psychiatric hospitals and labor camps.

4. It is at this point that the fourth contradiction in the position of the Soviet aristocracy becomes evident. The dissident intelligentsia will not help the aristocracy—both because of the egalitarian outlook that historically has shaped their consciousness and because of their scorn for such mendacious and perfidious *nouveaux riches*. The intelligentsia regards the aristocrats as the moral dregs of society, as a mob of gangsters whom an accident of history has enabled to grab power in a great country. (I myself could not avoid a feeling of rage and disgust when I visited the boyar countryseat that I described at the beginning of this study.)

But what does this division between aristocracy and intelligentsia mean in objective terms? The intelligentsia is the only element of the social system capable of generating the ideas needed by the system in order to function properly. The split—the "contradiction"—between the intelligentsia and the aristocracy therefore makes it impossible for the society to undergo the positive historical change that it needs today. Consequently, without mutual concessions both by the aristocracy (which must finally guarantee society a decent minimum level of human rights) and by the intelligentsia (which must assent to the privileges of the new "new class" in order to prevent the next GULAG and ensure society's historical progress), such a change is impossible.

However, this contradiction has already gone so far that its resolution is impossible without an arbiter whose authority is recognized equally by both sides. The Western intellectual community could serve as such an arbiter. It could work out a precise and detailed program to reconcile all the positive sociopolitical forces in the USSR—a program that would unite them in order to take a new step forward in history; that would provide for guarantees of privileges (for the positive segment of the elite), guarantees of the reconstruction of the economy (for the managerial class), and guarantees of elementary human rights (for the intelligentsia); and that would make it obvious that there is an indissoluble connection among all these elements of a positive social system—i.e., that would show clearly that the aristocratization of the elite is impossible without human rights and that a general reconstruction of the economy is impossible without political support from the elite as it becomes an aristocracy.

5. The most serious contradiction in the position of the Soviet

aristocracy is the contradiction with its partners in power. It is the most serious because there can be no positive resolution, no compromise; essentially this contradiction involves a fight to the death. It is no secret that the centrist group that now dominates the Politburo has prevailed not so much because of its political strength as because of the political weakness of its opponents, who have so far been unable to work out either a unified strategy for a restoration of Stalinism or a popular program, and have not found a leader with an aura of authority. This makes the present a unique moment in history, a time when the "right wing" forces could be defeated one by one. Unfortunately, as the events of the last few years have shown, Brezhnev's centrist group has proved incapable—by itself—of accomplishing this historic task.

E. THE POLITICAL RETREAT OF THE ARISTOCRACY

There are signs that the leaders of the centrist group sense how difficult their position is. It is indicated, specifically, by the policy of Detente they have proclaimed—an effort to prevent the sort of confrontation with the West which is needed by their opponents in order to force the regime to take a harder line inside the country and to strengthen the economic hegemony of the military-industrial complex. It is also indicated by many of Brezhnev's statements, if they are read from the standpoint of the "underlying meaning" commonly inferred in a society subject to censorship. (The art in this kind of communication consists in being able to set forth one's ideas in such a way that those for whom they are intended understand everything, while those against whom they are directed can find nothing to take offense at.)

Let us recall, for example, the atmosphere of the 24th CPSU Congress to help us understand the problem. In order to gain support for his program, which in essence was a course favoring above-average growth rates for Group B (light) industry, Brezhnev said the following on March 30, 1971:

> In charting this course, the Party proceeds . . . from the fact that the fullest possible satisfaction of people's material and cultural needs is an important aim of social production under socialism. . . . From the very first days of Soviet power our Party and state have done everything they could in this sphere.[6]

[6]See L. I. Brezhnev, *Official Report to the 24th Congress by the CPSU Central Committee* (Moscow, 1971), p. 50.

As is well known, Malenkov paid with his political life for his attempt to relate precisely what "our Party and government have done in this sphere." Brezhnev takes Malenkov's unhappy experience into account and pacifies his opponents with a ritual bow. "However," he goes on to say, "because of certain historical factors our opportunities have been limited." Brezhnev tries to put the essence of the artless "Malenkov Declaration" into this cautious euphemism, which enables him to take the next step: "Now they have been substantially broadened, and this gives the Party grounds for raising the question of orienting economic construction even more toward improving the life of the people."[7]

Now let us recall that 1977 has arrived and that last year (1976) at the 25th Congress "our Party" planned above-average growth for Group A (*heavy*) industry. Thus in 1971 "our opportunities" gave the Party grounds for "raising the question" of orienting economic activity toward "improving the life of the people," but in 1976—evidently—they no longer did so. What does this mean? Because of what new "historical factors" did the Party revise the course it solemnly proclaimed only five years before?

Since we have received no explanation, elementary logic leads us to conclude that the five-year period of "development" of the national economy did not *broaden* but rather *narrowed* "our opportunities." This means that either the economy is moving backward or . . . Brezhnev had to retreat from his "course" under pressure from superior forces. We know that the economy is making progress, however slow and contradictory; therefore, the second assumption must be the correct one. We can now uncover the real message being delivered by the speaker from his lofty rostrum. Let us return to Brezhnev's speech in 1971:

> The Party also proceeds from the fact that improving the working people's well-being is becoming a more and more urgent requirement for our economic development itself, one of the important economic prerequisites for the rapid growth of production.[8]

Let us translate this sentence into ordinary language. "You must finally realize," Brezhnev is saying to the Congress, "that we are not talking about humane considerations, but about the fact that the economic growth of the country that we rule has been stalled by the weakness of Group B—that it is impossible to develop production

[7] *Ibid.*

[8] *Ibid.*

further without raising the standard of living." In his coded Party jargon Brezhnev states the reasons for the need to emphasize light industry rather frankly:

> This shift stems not only from our line favoring the further enhancement of the role of material and moral work incentives. The question is a considerably broader one, . . . involving the development of society's main productive force.[9]

That is, given the current standard of living, the main productive force is ceasing to produce—therein lies the catastrophic danger of the lag in Group B, according to the Brezhnev of 1971.

Today's Brezhnev—at the 25th Congress—says nothing about this. By his silence he signals his listeners that this time he has been defeated, that his opponents' pressure has proven too much for him to withstand. If matters had gone no further at the 24th Congress, then the revision of the Party's course undertaken at the 25th Congress would not have been so obvious. But Brezhnev went further at the 24th Congress and drew practical conclusions. He raised his hand against the holy of holies—against the very function of Group A and even of the military-industrial complex. "Heavy industry," he said

> is to expand considerably its output of means of production for the accelerated development of agriculture, light industry, and the food industry and for the still greater development of housing construction, trade, and personal services for the population.[10]

This sounds very much like Malenkov, who long after his removal served as a target for the most vulgar satire; all the newspapers heaped scorn on his proposal that "defense plants manufacture saucepans." Suddenly the Party's General Secretary was speaking in this way from the rostrum of the Congress: it was a shock—and not only for the satirists. But Brezhnev went even further. He made a statement whose importance it is difficult to overestimate:

> Considering the high scientific and technical level of the defense industry, passing on its experience, inventions, and discoveries *to all spheres of the economy* is becoming a matter of paramount importance. [Emphasis added.]

That is practically a public scandal. After all, Brezhnev was essentially saying: Gentlemen of the military, the time has come for you

[9] *Ibid.*

[10] *Ibid.*, p. 56.

to share your privileges with light industry.

We should not fail to give Brezhnev his due for his courage at the time. He threw down the gauntlet to the military-industrial complex, and he attempted to enlist the support of the Congress for the destalinization of the Soviet economy and for restricting the military's exceptional position (essentially their dictatorship) in it. It is clear from what he went on to say that he was deliberately proposing a change in policy:

> In this connection, I would like to point out that 42 percent of the output produced by the defense industry already goes to meet civilian needs. [Nevertheless,] the Party is placing before heavy industry the task of expanding consumer goods production directly at its enterprises.

Brezhnev was attempting to "pay off" the Soviet people for the privileges of the Soviet aristocracy (and thereby resolve the first contradiction in the position of the new "new class"), but he could not bring it off!

Specialists know that not only this kind of language, but also the very spirit of economic destalinization had disappeared without a trace at the 25th Congress, and that Brezhnev's political retreat was plainly demonstrated. Of course, Brezhnev and the aristocratic group headed by him are resisting and striking counterblows. For the first time since Trotsky and Bulganin, the army is under the command of a civilian. Ustinov and Brezhnev himself have become marshals, and thus cut off the real military marshals' path into the Politburo. Calls for disarmament are becoming more and more persistent. But it is clear that these are rearguard actions—not offensive, but defensive moves. In his most recent speech in Rumania, Brezhnev declared:

> To continue or stop the arms race, to move on to disarmament or not—this is an issue too serious to be allowed to be decided by the bellicose generals *from the Pentagon and NATO* and by the *monopolies* that get rich by producing arms. This is a matter for responsible statesmen.[11]

Try substituting the words "from Frunze Street" and "ministries," respectively, for those that are italicized, and you will again get a coded message, this time addressed to the West:

> If you want to deal with "responsible statesmen," then help me abate the onslaught by my "bellicose generals," give me arguments

[11] *Pravda*, November 25, 1976. Emphases added.

> that carry weight to combat them. By approving a record budget for the Pentagon, you are giving *them* arguments—not me.

In this same speech (again for the first time since Malenkov), Brezhnev acknowledged that in case of war not capitalism alone, as earlier propaganda had asserted, but "mankind may be completely annihilated."

This is not merely a signal: it is an entreaty. It testifies to the weakness of the aristocratic faction of the Soviet leadership—to the fact that it is having great difficulty controlling events and that its ship is running into trouble in the "Bermuda Triangle" of Soviet politics. On the other hand, it does not indicate that the aristocracy has outlived its historical function, but rather testifies to the weakness of its present leaders, who are incapable (it has turned out) of carrying out structural economic reforms, of establishing a political alliance with the managerial class, of revising the concepts of the existing ideology, of reaching a compromise with the intelligentsia, and finally, of separating themselves politically from their opponents. Brezhnev, who is unquestionably a genius in dealing with the bureaucracy and a Grand Master of apparat intrigue, has proved to be weak as a *political* leader.

Of the Russian tsars, he most resembles Boris Godunov, also a phenomenal intriguer who had a visceral awareness of any threat to his personal power and managed to strike preventive blows, but, like Brezhnev, a very poor strategist. A leader of the caliber of Catherine the Great, not Boris Godunov, is needed to accomplish the substantial tasks that confront the aristocratic faction of the Soviet elite today and to effect the transition from the Petrine-Stalinist, elitist-squirearchal type of administration to the elitist-aristocratic type characteristic of Catherine's reign. Whether the Soviet aristocracy is capable of putting forward such a leader will become manifest in the future—after Brezhnev.

Postscript. The present work had been completed before I learned of the publication of I. Zemtsov, *Partiya ili mafiya? Razvorovannaya respublika* [Party or Mafia? The ravaged republic] (Paris: Les Editeurs Reunis, 1976), and V. Voynovich, *Ivan'kiada* (Ardis, 1976). The first of these books is the testimony of a former Soviet sociologist who recently emigrated to Israel; it has a wealth of factual material, but unfortunately the author often refers to sources that cannot be checked. The second is a piece of involuntary social research done by a well-known Soviet writer living in Moscow, using the method of participant observation.

I was struck by the degree to which both of these authors confirm many of the points made in my analysis. For example, if we are to believe Zemtsov, the speed of the "migration to academe" by the Party and state "nomenklatura" in some union republics has exceeded my wildest expectations; by 1969 *more than half* of all these cadres held academic titles. In the Baltic republics academic titles were held by 62 percent of the republic Central Committee "nomenklatura" and 59 percent of the Council of Ministers "nomenklatura." The corresponding figures for Central Asia were 58 and 56 percent, and for Georgia and Armenia taken together, 71 and 73 percent. The proportions in Azerbaydzhan in 1966 were 67 and 63 percent.

The revelations of Voynovich's book are even more significant. He relates an episode from everyday life, for example, that captures in miniature the nature of the social conflict in the USSR today. The main protagonist, Ivan'ko, is a Party bureaucrat assigned to "official literary work" and a typical representative of the new "new class." He lives in Russia only in the physical sense, so to speak; his soul belongs to the West, where he has acquired some unbelievable appliances for his apartment and dreams of someday acquiring a "stereophonic toilet," as Voynovich puts it. To understand the present stage of mental development of the Soviet aristocracy, all you need to know is Ivan'ko's life's dream, along with the fact that he not only does not try to find a common language with the author, who represents the Soviet intelligentsia and dissenters, but on the contrary gets into a stupid, angry squabble with him over an apartment. At the same time, Voynovich shows that he himself will not make an effort to cooperate with Ivan'ko under any circumstances: his loathing is too much to overcome. But given the fact that Ivan'ko wants a stereophonic toilet, is it likely that he wants a world war? Does he want a new Stalin, who would make it his first order of business to declare Ivan'ko a cosmopolitan and his stereophonic toilet an instrument of American subversion, and who would ship him off to someplace where there are no toilets at all?

Chapter II

POLITICAL PORTRAIT OF A SOVIET MANAGER

A. A BOSS AND HIS BOSSES

The scene is Leningrad, 1973. My interlocutor is in his late fifties. He is a tall man with sharp features, tastefully dressed, with a decidedly authoritative, even somewhat arrogant manner. The word "boss" seems to be written in big letters on his face. To his subordinates he speaks laconically and with mild irony. He solves problems that seem to them unusually complex with a single sentence; he cuts through them in the same way Alexander cut through the Gordian knot. It seems that he has an answer ready for everything, that he has foreseen his subordinates' questions. He is undoubtedly a person of authority, and the cult of personality permeates the office. I can feel it in every pore of my skin—the skin of a writer. But it is not merely respect for rank: it is also admiration by his subordinates for the man who is unquestionably their superior in intelligence, experience, and competence. I am in the office of the general director of a large machine-building association. It happens that I have come at a dramatic moment, when a shortage of a generally scarce raw material threatens to halt the operations of the gigantic casting shop. A suspension of operations will mean idleness for almost 1,500 workers, a situation that is among the most dangerous in Soviet industry.

What does a high-ranking manager do in such a situation? He makes phone calls. He picks up the receiver of the "vertushka" and makes a call.[1] The general director makes his calls strictly in accordance with the hierarchy. He first calls the first secretary of the borough Party committee; then a province Party committee instructor; then the assistant head of the province committee's department

[1] The "vertushka" is a special "nomenklatura" telephone that operates at high frequencies. It is installed only in the offices of high officials and in the apartments of Politburo members, the top officials in the apparatus, and the first secretaries of the province Party committees. It is the only form of communication in the USSR that is not subjected to censorship or wiretapping. It is, if you will, a symbol of the political supremacy of the post-Stalin "nomenklatura" over the post-Stalin KGB.

of machine building; then the head of the department; then the province committee's secretary for industry. This goes on for more than an hour. The general director has to explain the entire situation to each one from the beginning. He has to appeal to each one humbly: "Help; this is an emergency; SOS!" He has to listen to caustic questions from each one: "What were you thinking about before? Why have you let matters go to the last extremity? To the point of a scandal? To the point of stopping production?" He has to make excuses to each one in a detailed and humiliating manner: "Our suppliers have let us down. According to the plan they were supposed to deliver the raw materials a month ago. We sent telegrams, complained to the ministry and the State Planning Committee, sent a representative (a prodder, as he is called in the semi-official jargon) to Moscow and another to our suppliers, and did everything that is supposed to be done in such cases—to no avail. Now we are faced with a catastrophe."

For one hour this superman, who is accustomed to commanding tens of thousands of people, had his nose rubbed in the dirt no less than six times, as a correspondent from the capital sat watching. He was boiling; his face gradually grew flushed. After he had spoken to one of the instructors he muttered in a fury: "Oh, what a scoundrel. I wouldn't even hire him as a stock clerk! He's a nonentity, but he flings taunts like a big shot. . . ." But he had to make the calls. Otherwise heads would roll, and his would be the first.

Why was he calling all these officials? To "rob" someone (again semi-official jargon), it turns out: some cardboard factory or pulp and paper mill—in short, someone from Group B. Using the "vertushka," it is possible to obtain official permission for an unofficial "robbery." What is involved is the compulsory withdrawal of raw materials in short supply from enterprises that produce consumer goods. The consumer can wait; nothing will happen to him if he "underreceives" (also jargon) his dippers or slippers. This logic is known to everyone. People always talk about it ironically: the "robbery" of light industry that takes place daily and on a nationwide scale has been legitimized; one might even call it sacred.

What is the mechanism by which this robbery is carried out? That is what occupied me during those stormy hours as I sat in the general director's office and he made his phone calls. The secretary of the borough committee could not help him: the borough had none of the needed raw material. The province committee officials could have helped if there had been any of the material within the boundaries of the province and provided that (here the most interesting part begins) there were no other claimants with a higher "heavyweight" ranking. The trouble was that my general director was too late: all the cardboard factories in the province had already been robbed. In any case, he was *told* that he was too late.

It turns out that the rights of the mafiosi from Group A are unequal. It goes without saying that the military possesses the *jus primo noctis*, so to speak;[2] but who takes precedence after the military? This is where the realm of arbitrariness begins. If we are talking about Leningrad, the Kirov Plant is a top-level mafioso; it is a "heavyweight." Its general director has a direct entree to Moscow and the Central Committee, and it is dangerous to offend him.

In what order are ordinary "middleweights" ranked in this hierarchy of robbers? In no order, for no established hierarchy exists. Everything depends on how close you are personally to the province committee officials. Unfortunately, our general director is too aristocratic and does not like to drink vodka with the province committee rabble; that I realized at once. Furthermore, his association is not the Kirov Plant or its equivalent; it is definitely a "middleweight." Perhaps that is the reason that none of the province committee officials helped his association. How can he be sure? What is the association to do now?

There is only one way out: once again a phone call is required. This time it is necessary to call the Master himself (the first secretary of the province committee). He is the only person who has the authority and power to order an all-union dragnet, so to speak, for scarce raw materials. He alone can call—using the same all-powerful "vertushka"—the Masters of other provinces and offer them a deal. He always has in reserve some raw material that is in short supply in another province, and there is always an opportunity to exchange it for what "his enterprises" need at any given time. This makes it clearly evident who bears the final responsibility, so to speak, for the fate of industry in the province, for the life or death of any of its enterprises—in other words, who is their actual *owner*. It is the first secretary of the province committee—the local embodiment of the Party's universal will—who exercises supreme control over the local economic empire, who really *answers* for the normal functioning of the empire. He answers for it with his enormous *political capital*. He makes deals for which the OBKhSS would put an ordinary manager

[2]There are many military enterprises in Leningrad, and just as the Party apparatus holds indisputable sway over political life, the military-industrial complex exercises indisputable dictatorship over production.

into prison for seven to ten years. But the OBKhSS cannot touch him. He is the Master; he is the owner; the OBKhSS works for *him*. Managers and directors, even general directors, also work for him: they are essentially no more than his stewards, his agents, who possess only the right to give orders. In order to carry out his proprietary function, the first secretary of the province party committee must have at his disposal a rather large economic apparatus. He has to know what is needed, by whom and where—on an all-union scale—and he must have specific reserves. He has to know whom to call, how—and through whom—to arrange things, etc., because this involves exchanging not only goods, but also connections, influence, and prestige.

So the general director calls the Master. Once again he explains everything from the very beginning. Once again he listens to reproaches and threats. Once again he is humiliated. It is as if the receiver has gotten red-hot and is burning his fingers. Indeed, he is being made a scapegoat. Where is the vaunted centralized management and supply now? Why has it subjected him to this torture by humiliation? Why has it forced him to beg for what the enterprise is entitled to according to law and the plan? What kind of a system is this that turns a captain of industry into a beggar at the church door? What kind of a system is this that serves to cover up chaos and arbitrariness?

You can well imagine that my enraged interlocutor hurled all these questions at me.[3] It is hardly surprising: we had been made so tense by the irrationality of what was happening, my interlocutor was so upset by the humiliation that he had just had to undergo, and I was so discomposed by his agitation that a singular type of catharsis, to use Aristotelian terminology, inevitably had to take place. It was as if we opened our hearts to one another. We forgot about being guarded and diplomatic toward one another, forgot that we hardly knew each other. We began to talk with such frankness about subjects that went so far beyond the incident we had experienced that this conversation, at least for me, proved

[3]I happened to be in his office essentially by chance, simply because the editor-in-chief of the journal *Voprosy literatury*, wearied by the literary critics' interminable discussions of today's Soviet manager, decided that he wanted at last a realistic portrait of a captain of Soviet industry. But I turned out to be a "painter of seascapes" rather than a portrait painter. The portrait that I ended up with was not so much a picture of the captain as of his ship, or of the Soviet seas through which it must plow, running with the waves. On the matter of Soviet discussions regarding today's manager, see the Spring 1973 issue of *Soviet Studies in Philosophy*, which is devoted to such a discussion.

to be extraordinarily important.

In the picture drawn by my interlocutor, it is as if the Soviet socialist enterprise stands at the intersection of two lines of arbitrariness. The first—vertical arbitrariness—comes from the central apparatus of the State Planning Committee and the ministry, which "hand down" plans and allocation orders to the enterprise. The arbitrariness lies in the fact that, depending on personal relationships, the plan handed down to the enterprise can be large or small in scale, the output assortment can be advantageous or disadvantageous for the enterprise, its output may or may not be exported (considerable amounts of "extra pay" depend on this), etc. But arbitrariness is manifested above all in which suppliers are chosen for the enterprise—good ones or bad ones. Sometimes one can be stuck with suppliers with whom one can never fulfill the plan. That is when one can easily fall prey to the second line of arbitrariness, which leads from the local Party apparatus—the horizontal line of arbitrariness.

Total dependence on officials who have different degrees of responsibility but are equally incompetent, the necessity of constantly humbling himself before people to whom he, the director, is only a pawn in their own careerist game—that is what enraged my general director more than anything else. He functions in a situation of constant, chronic, unresolvable conflict—both with local officials and those in Moscow.

But this was not the thing that most interested me—rather it was what seemed to me the obvious contradiction in his own position as one of the mafiosi, one of the "robbers" of light industry. What could he undertake without this Party apparatus which he and others like him had essentially turned into an apparatus for handling supply and the organized robbery of Group B? If someone were to take away his "vertushka" and the little book containing the telephone numbers of the "nomenklatura," which are his only weapons in the fight for survival, he would be ruined, he would go under; is that not so? In other words, he has survived only because of that apparatus, which, even though it humiliates him, will save him from ruin in the end. He ought to be blessing the Party apparatus rather than cursing it.

My interlocutor countered by asking if it is not the Party apparatus itself that has created this chaotic economic universe, which cannot function without the compulsory distribution of allocation orders and periodic Tatar raids on light industry by heavy industry, and which essentially transforms him from an economic strategist into a supply worker. And not just him alone, but all the province committee officials and even the Master himself, the first secretary. Does that make sense? Would it not be easier for him, and for everyone else, if he could simply buy his raw materials from stores, or choose his suppliers himself, or produce the raw materials himself? The entire pyramid, the entire hierarchy of dependencies, would collapse at once, and he could take care of his business and the secretary of the province committee could take care of *his*.

This seemingly obvious assumption involved one little presupposition that my interlocutor had failed to take into account. It presupposed that the secretary of the province committee has *his own business*, other than being the managers' master. Taking away the province committee secretary's right to run the province's economy is the same as reducing him from general to buck private. The reason that he needs economic chaos, which dooms the country to stagnation, is that it is precisely this chaos that makes him a superarbiter, a general intermediary among the managers. If everything becomes simple, logical, and orderly, and the managers begin to work with one another *directly*, then the province committee secretary's function will disappear along with the present artificial complexity.

The situation paradoxically resembles the one that confronted Luther in the sixteenth century: Does a person need an intermediary in his communion with God? If not, then why should the church exist? Why have a gigantic organization that carries out this mediation, on which it bases its claim to temporal and even universal supremacy? Is it not the case that the Party apparatus is simply a broker which has appropriated to itself a powerful intermediary function and has turned this function into an instrument of actual domination? Therefore, I declared to the director, what seems like chaos to you is divine harmony to the secretary of the province committee.

B. THE TECHNOSTRUCTURE AND POLITICS

As you might guess, having touched upon the subject of Luther, we soon found ourselves confronting the problem of a reformation (an economic reformation, of course). My interlocutor not only agreed with me, but proved to be far more radical than I. In fact, he declared, we are confronted by the need for a revolution. Not a violent and bloody revolution, fraught with the danger of civil war; after all, the meaning of a revolution does not have to do with blood, but rather—as Lenin said—with the question of power and the question of ownership. To whom do the productive forces rightly belong? To whom does the right to make strategic decisions belong? To which class? To the class of intermediaries, administrators, Party clerks, and bureaucratic bigwigs? Or to the class of managers who run production in practice? It is perfectly clear to me, said the director, that the existing system of economic management arose during Stalin's time. It arose because of Soviet power's lack of confidence in the managers of that period, who could have been bourgeois specialists—or ignorant and freewheeling proletarians singled out for advancement. At that time it was necessary to concentrate supreme control over the economy in the hands of "the initiated," trusted people, who were of course Party cadres. But now, in the era of the scientific and technical revolution, when competence is everything and the most competent cadres are not sitting in Party or ministry offices but are at the enterprises, now everything has changed. Now we—the managers—are "the initiated," and *we* do not have confidence in the incompetent Party cadres; their economic authority has become an anachronism. The conclusion is simple. The alignment of social forces has changed, and the center of gravity of social responsibility has shifted to the enterprises. In other words, there has been a change in production relations, in the base; accordingly, there should be a change in the superstructure. Isn't that what the Marxist law of social development tells us?[4]

[4]According to Jerry F. Hough's classic scheme (presented in *The Soviet Prefects* [Cambridge, Mass.: Harvard University Press, 1969]), the Soviet economy has proved to be stable and generally manageable because at the local level the "vertical line" of the ministry bureaucracies intersects the coordinating "horizontal line" of Party organizers (the prefects), which is essentially a substitute for the organizing function of the market under the conditions of a rigidly centralized economy. That was probably true from the 1930's to the 1950's. But a new phenomenon has emerged in the Soviet economy since the 1960's—namely, a second "horizontal line" representing the managers, which parallels the "horizontal line" of economic management by the Party and seeks to perform the same function of organizing the economy. This new stratum has evidently been a factor in slowing down the growth rate of the Soviet economy because the two "horizontal lines" are competing against one another, which has made the Soviet economy less rather than more manageable. The main problem that confronts the country's leaders today is to decide which of these lines they ultimately intend to rely on in the country's further economic development. Reliance on the "horizontal line" of *prefects* is characteristic of the Stalinist economic structure. Reliance on the "horizontal line" of *managers* would mean the destalinization of the economy, the introduction of at least a limited market, and perhaps something like the NEP, which is precisely the goal that the post-Stalin leadership has been striving toward, but has been unable to achieve.

That was the logic of my interlocutor's reasoning. Whether or not it was Marxist, one thing was obvious: it reflected an absolutely unequivocal desire to "share the burden" of political power in the country. In this regard, he declared that it was not at all a matter of his personal craving for power, but a matter of necessity stemming from the realities of the new social differentiation in the country. He led me to understand that he was only a representative of a certain social group: he made reference to those who stand "behind him"—the engineers, economists, sociologists, and managers which make up his staff (or as he put it, the technostructure). According to him, these are independent and in many respects brilliant people who think rationally and in broad terms; they had gathered around him because of the establishment of the associations, which are a form of symbiosis of factories and scientific institutes. These people have become accustomed to thinking independently, and they want to work independently to solve the production and social problems confronting industry. They are caught up by the idea of the technological revolution. They are ashamed of Soviet backwardness, its dependence on foreign technology, its humiliation. They believe that the reason for this backwardness is that their hands are tied—and tied tightly. Give them free rein, and tomorrow they will fire half the workers in their shops and pay the rest two, three, or five times more, depending on their skills (this assures them of sympathy and support from the skilled segment of the working class); they will introduce innovative, fundamentally new modes of work organization; they will be ready to experiment day and night. To them this is a matter of destiny, of self-affirmation, of realizing fully their human potential; in other words, it involves the meaning of life. They are seething with a desire for activity, and they believe that given a free rein they could not only reach, but even surpass by a wide margin, the so-called world standards for labor productivity—that they could make Russia a leader of world scientific and technical progress and, incidentally, a provider of food for starving peoples. Of course they are not thinking in terms of Khrushchev's amateurish schemes, which were (so to speak) the products of a revolutionary-bureaucratic mentality. They are thinking in terms of a realistic and effective strategy of "reconstruction," whose elaboration will inevitably engage the energies of all those who take an active part in the country's intellectual life. In the minds of my young people, the general director said, the only obstacle is the Party administration's total domination of the economy.

My interlocutor attempted to support this viewpoint with his own sociological observations—in particular, his observations regarding the system of social selection that has arisen in the country during the past decade. In his opinion, all of today's educated young people who have spirit and think for themselves are going either into science and production or into the open opposition, into the dissident movement. Those who become Party cadres today are generally either people who are hopelessly mediocre and intellectually and spiritually dead or those who value power as an end in itself. Thus, to the subordinates who make up his technostructure, the basic social conflict in Russia today stems from the fact that the mediocre hold sway over the gifted, that gray and faceless people hold sway over enthusiasts, that the dead hold sway over the living. That is why the social conflict is developing, *must* develop (in the general director's opinion) into a political struggle.

During the ten years of my itinerant life as a journalist, in the course of which (to my surprise) I had managed to traverse half the country, I had probably gotten to know the Soviet technostructure as well as my interlocutor. I knew that it was indeed seething with a desire for activity and power, and I even undertook a discreet survey in an attempt to determine, if only approximately, the proportion of contemporary directors who are striving for independence and political influence. In interviews with five of these directors, I asked them to estimate the percentage of directors they believed were seeking to participate actively in a "reconstruction" of the Soviet economy. In four of the five cases, the directors' estimates were the same—30 percent; in the fifth case the estimate was 25 percent. I knew all this, but. . . .

At this point I attempted to bring my interlocutor back to Luther's situation. If the "church" already exists, if it holds strong positions, if it has an organization and all the key posts are in its hands, it will not voluntarily surrender its role, no matter how many times Marx or the holy scriptures are quoted. Sacred writings are "sacred" for it only until it has to defend its real interests. It is impossible to *persuade* it to relinquish power: strength is needed. Where is this strength? Luther could not have triumphed if he had relied solely on the Bible. He triumphed because he relied on the sword of the German princes and the financial might of the urban burghers. Where is your sword, and what constitutes your might?

C. THE NEW STRUCTURE OF POWER

My interlocutor answered my question with a question: Why do you think that *none* of the leaders since Stalin, without a single exception—Malenkov, Khrushchev, Kosygin, and Brezhnev—has continued the Stalinist economic regime, with its orientation solely toward building up military might and achieving extraordinary political objectives? Why have they, on the contrary, attempted in one way or another to restructure the economy by orienting it toward satisfying society's needs as well? The results have not been very substantial, but in this case what is of interest is not results, but intentions. Therefore, we shall make the question more precise: Why have these intentions of satisfying society's needs, rather than the opposite ones, dominated the actions of the post-Stalin leadership?

I have tried to answer this question many times—not only during that conversation with the general director, but also in practically everything that I wrote in Moscow and write now. Neither my interlocutor nor I was satisfied with the stereotyped fatalistic or, if you will, technical-economic answer. Neither he nor I believed that it all comes down to the increased complexity of the present-day economy or to its greater scale, which (it is said) is inherently incompatible with forced labor. It was believed as long ago as the fifth century that forced labor had outlived its usefulness, which did not keep Stalin from reviving it in the twentieth—in an economy incomparably more complex—and even achieving on this basis the fundamental modernization of the Russian economic system. No; the answer, in my view, is far more complex. It lies not in the economic sphere, but rather in the social essence of the post-Stalin system—or to be more precise, in the processes of social differentiation mentioned by my interlocutor. However, unlike him, I find that this differentiation has proceeded rapidly not only in society as a whole, but also deep inside the "new class" that rules the country. Fundamental models of behavior have changed. The hypocritically puritanical model, oriented toward the figure of the ascetic soldier-leader sleeping on a barracks cot, has given way to an undisguised craving for wealth and privileges, oriented toward the figure of the stolid leader-bourgeois, a sort of Soviet Louis Philippe who collects automobiles.[5] The question arises of how to square these glaringly obvious privileges with the people's egalitarian culture and with the egalitarian ideology that provides the mandate under which this

[5] See Chapter I above, esp. pp. 1-5.

"new class" that wants so badly to live by bourgeois standards rules the country.

The only resolution of this contradiction, which in the opinion of my interlocutor was intuitively recognized by the post-Stalin leaders, is to *buy off* the people by providing them with food, clothing, and shoes, solving their housing problem, giving them automobiles—in short, by turning them into bourgeois and giving them the opportunity to have a European standard of living, so that in the new social system they too would have something to lose, so that the privileges of the "new class" would not be so striking, and so that the issue would become only the degree of privilege rather than the very existence of illegal privilege in a country of semi-Asiatic poverty.[6]

Of course the emergence of the new "new class" is by no means the only sociopolitical process that has been taking place in the country during the past twenty years. Intertwined with it has been the process, so to speak, of the redisposition of ownership—a peculiar sort of decentralization of ownership. It is axiomatic that in essence the 20th Congress (1956) constituted successful rebellion by the political machine (the Party) against the police machine (the MVD [Ministry of Internal Affairs])—i.e., the disintegration of the Stalinist, two-headed system of administration. It is less obvious that those who gained most from this were the local Party satraps—the local Party administration, to use my interlocutor's term. At their own level—the province and republic level—they did not permit any "20th Congress," any "collective leadership," any oligarchy, and in essence they became the sole masters of the regions under their authority (little Stalins, so to speak), so that the entire Soviet system of administration proved to be fundamentally a dual system, with an oligarchy at the top and tyranny below.[7] In Stalin's time the local

[6]In her very interesting book *In Stalin's Time* (London: Oxford University Press, 1976), Vera S. Dunham raises a crucial question regarding the conditions for the functioning of the postwar elite. She reasonably assumes and superbly demonstrates (by means of examples from literature) the existence of what she calls the "Big Deal"—i.e., a tacit agreement between society's ruling clique and the top segment of the so-called "middle class" that has essentially meant *bribing* a certain stratum in order to create a new social base for totalitarian dictatorship. In the post-totalitarian phase of development of Soviet society, however, this "deal," once big, has apparently turned out to be not big enough. What is needed now is, if you will, a *new* "Big Deal" on a far more massive scale, which will make it possible for the elite to change the very nature of the Soviet regime.

[7]I spoke about this in greater detail at the Third Williamsburg Conference; see "The Soviet Union: Society and Policy" (Center for Strategic and International Studies, Georgetown University, 1976), pp. 35-36.

apparatchiki were merely overseers, unquestioningly carrying out the economic will of the central administration. Their management and coordination function was restricted not only from above, but also horizontally by the local MVD agencies that held sway over them. After Stalin's death the situation changed in a fundamental way: on the one hand, the domination of the police agencies was ended, and on the other hand, it became possible for the local apparatchiki to have an influence on the central economic administration. In many cases they have even proved strong enough to impose on it their own counterplans, and to a certain extent they have substituted direct relationships among themselves for the once omnipotent Committee for Material and Technical Supply. They not only *feel* that they are masters of their satrapies: to a considerable extent they have become the masters. If we take ownership to mean responsibility for the life and death of enterprises, then it could be said that these little Stalins acquired ownership in place of the big Stalin they lost.

These processes have made the present ruling group heterogeneous. It is not a monolithic party that is in power, but an unstable coalition, a bloc, if one may put it this way, of various embryonic political parties with different and even opposing interests. In this bloc the central Party-bureaucratic administration represents the proto-aristocratic party of the "new class," the party that has an interest in reconstructing the economy. The local administrations represent the new owners of production; they will not permit any reconstruction that could encroach on their proprietary interests.

But the main strength of the local administrators lies not so much in their economic role as in their political role—in the fact that in the Soviet parliament, the Plenum of the Party Central Committee, the ruling bloc parties are unequally represented. While the party of the central bureaucracy (which should not be confused with the central economic apparatus) controls less than 30 percent of the votes, the party of the little Stalins has 40-45 percent. This puts the central bureaucracy's plans for reconstructing the economy under the strict control of the Stalinist parliamentary majority, which is the basis of all the contradictions and all the crosscurrents of Brezhnev's administration in both domestic and foreign policy.

D. A MANAGERS' REVOLUTION?

The answer to my rhetorical question—Where is the managers' sword, and what constitutes their might?—follows from this analysis. Their might lies in the fact that (1) the aims of the central administration party in the ruling bloc coincide with their own, (2) the faction of the Party elite seeking to become an aristocracy will never achieve its aims if it does not enter into an alliance with them, and the elite faction needs a strong and independent managerial base as a condition of its further existence, for no one else will be able to pay off the people for the privileges of the aristocracy. In any case, the elite faction's present allies—the little Stalins—have furnished exhaustive proof of their complete inability during the twenty years of their economic supremacy. The little Stalins are bankrupts, and dangerous bankrupts at that; they are not only tying the hands of the central administration, but even threatening its very existence.

Take three seemingly quite simple questions. First: For fifteen years the commission on drawing up a new Constitution has been meeting, and for fifteen years it has been as unproductive as a Biblical fig tree. Thus for fifteen years the country has essentially been without a Constitution. *Why*? Let us assume that in this case the stumbling block is the difficulty of reconciling democratic maxims with the open persecution of dissenters. How then are we to answer the second question? Everyone knows that Khrushchev's Party program long ago became an underground document: it has been withdrawn from circulation, and quoting from it is forbidden. Thus for more than a decade the Party has essentially gone without a program. *Why*? And how are we to answer the third question? During all the years since Stalin's death, solemn incantations regarding the need to end at once the scattering of capital investments, concentrate on key projects, etc. have resounded from the rostrum of every congress and plenum. Year after year, five-year plan after five-year plan, the programs adopted by the State Planning Committee call for concentrating investments. The Committee's decisions, as is well known, are not merely forecasts: they have the force of law. But year after year, with equal persistence, these laws are violated under the noses of the Party and the government. In other words, the Soviet economy has proved to be incapable of acting according to its own laws. *Why*?

It seems to me that these failures are only symptoms of the latent but irreconcilable contradiction that is tearing apart the ruling bloc. The central administration, compelled to somehow reckon with world public opinion, Detente, and the European communist movement, has an interest in putting certain formulations in the Constitution and the Party program, while its "right-wing" allies have an interest in others. The central administration has an interest in concentrating capital investments, while the little Stalins have an interest in scattering them. The central administration needs Helsinkis while the "rightists" need Angolas.

Does it not follow from all this that the central administration—provided, of course, that it manages to perceive correctly its own interests—must propose a partnership to the managers? In other words, should not the revolution of 1956, which transferred ownership from the central administration to the little Stalins, be followed by a new revolution that will transfer ownership from the little Stalins to the managers? Will that not be the very managers' revolution dreamed of by my interlocutor?

The managers do not seek to overthrow the existing regime: they merely want to redistribute power within the regime—or what amounts to the same thing, to redistribute the votes in the Party parliament. Whereas now, let us assume, they have no more than 3 percent of the votes, they seek 30 percent, which together with the votes of the central administration's representatives would assure the new political bloc an absolute majority and predominance over the little Stalins. Of course, like everything else in the USSR today, this has a strange, ephemeral, and mystifying quality: the parliament is not a parliament as people generally conceive it, and the parties are not parties. On the other hand, interests are interests, and coalitions of interests are real political coalitions. We are not, therefore, talking about the institution of a democratic regime, but only the creation of the *political* prerequisites for reconstructing the economy for which the *social* prerequisites (as we have seen) have already been created during the twenty years since the tyrant's death. We are talking about the necessity of eliminating the threat of a restoration of Stalinism, about beginning to move the country *in the direction* of democracy instead of having it move in the opposite direction. This is not an abstract question, nor a noble wish: for the central administration, it is a question of its fate. It is the central administration that must break up the unreliable and dangerous coalition with the little Stalins, which is completely blocking any forward movement, and form a bloc with the managers in order to bring the structure of the country's political leadership into at least rough conformity with its social structure. Otherwise, the central administration will simply flounder in a swamp of inertia, dooming the country to stagnation and itself to waiting for the cataclysm.

E. THE POLITICAL POTENTIALITIES OF THE ASSOCIATIONS

Strange as it may seem, I think that there are some grounds for assuming that the central administration itself has begun to realize the need to form a bloc with the managers. I refer again to Brezhnev's official report to the 24th Party Congress. A good bit—one might even say the heart—of this report is devoted to the problem of production associations. The necessity of creating them was substantiated in a very detailed manner—both in theory and in practical terms.[8] Is it not clear from this that the General Secretary must have viewed this as a political rather than as an administrative problem? If not, it would have been solvable in the course of handling normal business, so to speak. If what was actually involved was merely combining certain plants with certain institutes, this problem would have belonged in *Literaturnaya gazeta* or, at best, in *Voprosy ekonomiki*, but certainly not in the political report to the Congress. It is another matter that you will not find anything like this in Brezhnev's report five years later at the 25th Congress. Brezhnev had retreated, and he could not help but retreat, given the makeup of his parliament.[9] True, two thousand associations have been established in Soviet industry, but their establishment represents only an administrative and technical innovation. In terms of what really matters, in terms of politics, they do not exist—much promise, but little in the way of results.

However, Brezhnev will not last forever. What he did not manage to accomplish might be brought off by his successor. There-

[8]His actual words were as follows: "In order to speed up the scientific and technical revolution, it is important to improve the forms of industrial organization by setting up production in a manner that meets current requirements. . . . All this is within the capability only of large associations. . . . The experience that has been amassed shows that only large associations are capable of bringing together an adequate number of qualified specialists and ensuring rapid technical progress (scientific and technical progress is the primary instrument for creating the material and technical foundation of communism). . . . The policy of establishing associations and combines must be pursued more resolutely, for in the long run they are to become the principal economically accountable units of social production. When establishing associations it is especially important to see to it that administrative boundaries and departmental subordination do not block the introduction of more effective forms of management" (Brezhnev, *Report to the 24th Congress*, pp. 69-70, 84). In short, the General Secretary was trying to keep both the prefects and the ministers from interfering with the associations.

[9]Perhaps that is why Shevardnadze, First Secretary of the Georgian Central Committee and *enfant terrible* of the Soviet leadership, speaking at the 25th Congress of the Georgian Communist Party (see *Zarya Vostoka*, January 23, 1976), for the first time in the Soviet press openly called for *renewal* of the Central Committee by bringing in "new people whose activities really involve them in life and who will bring new attitudes, new thoughts and ideas to the Central Committee."

fore, I think that it is worthwhile to examine the sociopolitical potentialities of production associations and determine how, in the opinion of my interlocutor and his "technostructure," they were originally conceived.

Let us imagine gigantic economic empires, similar to Ford's in the 1920's, that incorporate all production processes, beginning with the mining of raw materials and ending with project planning and scientific research institutes. All this is run by an independent "technostructure"—i.e., a group of managers headed by my interlocutor. What socioeconomic and political consequences would ensue if the development of such empires were the "general line of the Party"?

1. Simply because of its all-encompassing production structure, an industrial empire of this kind must go beyond the bounds of the regions governed by the first secretaries of the province Party committees.[10] It will be an interprovince entity, which means that it does away with what my interlocutor called the realm of horizontal arbitrariness. At the same time it eliminates the "robbery" of Group B enterprises and compulsory redistribution of their stocks within Group A, which is a practice engendered by this arbitrariness.

2. An empire of this kind will not fit within the framework of a single ministry: it will be interdepartmental, and will thus eliminate the sphere of vertical arbitrariness.[11] No longer will anyone be able to dictate to the "technostructure" modes of work organization or the pay of workers, or to thrust suppliers on it. It will have its own raw materials, reserves, funds and even—in place of "prodders"—its own lobby in parliament. In other words, it will defend its interests not in ministry corridors or the little Stalins' anterooms, not by begging for scarce raw materials, or spare parts, or project plans from its supplier firms, but directly before the country's supreme body.

3. Such an industrial empire will enter into direct relationships with its foreign counterparts, which could literally turn Detente upside down. The state's foreign trade monopoly is certainly no obstacle; after all, the associations are state organizations. Just as the associations will no longer require the mediation of the province committee secretaries, their need for the mediation of a special ministry will simply fade away. The foreign trade monopoly does not mean a monopoly for the Ministry of Foreign Trade, as Academician Inozemtsev, a counselor to Brezhnev, said at one of the Plenums of

[10]I.e., beyond what Brezhnev in his report euphemistically termed "administrative boundaries."

[11]I.e., what Brezhnev called "departmental subordination."

the Central Committee.[12] Thus, the "technostructure" will gain direct access to the sources of modernization, will pursue the technical policy that is in line with its competence, and will be able truly to open up the country to the exchange of information and contacts. This process of rationalizing the economy cannot fail to have a rationalizing effect on the country's entire public life.

4. Roughly speaking, the foundation of today's indisputable dictatorship of the military-industrial complex—on the administrative and technical plane rather than the strategic and cultural—is the rigid centralization of industrial management, which paradoxically, like everything else in the post-Stalin USSR, coexists with decentralized ownership. This centralization makes possible the unhindered pumping of resources from Group B to Group A, as well as from one sector to another within Group A. Will this be possible if the "technostructure" heads its own empires? Will they then hand over their raw materials, reserves, and stocks to the military? In the opinion of my interlocutor, that is unthinkable. The military-industrial complex will run into an impenetrable wall composed of the interests of the individual empires, and that will initiate the process of demilitarizing the economy, which will be more salutary for public life than any antiwar propaganda.

5. Inevitably, such dramatic changes in the organization of industrial management are impossible without related political and social changes. The political adjustments can be taken care of by placing a sufficient number of general directors, masters of the new industrial empires, in the parliament to break the resistance of the obsolescent classes, so to speak. By the latter, I mean the "horizontal" prefects, who at the critical moment will be able to form a bloc with their long-standing "vertical" enemies, the ministers. The bloc of the little Stalins and the central economic bureaucracy (which now has almost 20 percent of the votes in the Plenum), perhaps in combination with the military (another 7-8 percent), is the force that will have to be fought in the parliamentary arena. In addition to everything else, this could initiate open political struggle, instead of the present scrapping of bulldogs behind the drapes, which would

[12]Brezhnev himself spoke about this subject with extreme caution in his own report to the 24th Congress: "Enhancing the role of economic and scientific and technical ties with other countries will naturally require eliminating the narrow departmental approach to this important matter" (Brezhnev, *Official Report . . . 24th Congress*, p. 76). Since the USSR's "economic ties with other countries" are handled essentially by the Ministry of Foreign Trade, eliminating the "narrow departmental approach" can only mean eliminating that ministry's dictatorship in the sphere of foreign trade.

also have a salutary effect on the public atmosphere in the country.

6. The final thing that would ensue from a "general Party line" oriented toward associations is an advance in the sphere of social responsibility. What is now the most subtle argument put forward by advocates of the existing system? If Ford had gone bankrupt in the 1920's, they say, he would have answered for it with all his property. If Gregory Romanov brings his Leningrad industrial domain to the point of bankruptcy, he can answer for it with all his *political capital*—his place at the top of the hierarchy, his power, and an income that today's "technostructure" has not even dreamt of. Perhaps one of the secrets of the viability of what would appear to be an unviable economic system lies in the fact that it has managed to come up with this *substitution* for responsibility—that political capital has proved to be more or less comparable in this sense to financial capital. The "technostructure" has nothing with which to answer for failure, except perhaps its earnings, which cannot compare with the capital entrusted to it. All this would change if it were directing the new economic empires, for the right to run such complexes constitutes tremendous *administrative capital* that is not inferior to Ford's financial capital or Romanov's political capital. It means power, a position in the hierarchy, and an enormous income; in short, it means a real opportunity to assume responsibility for the fate of the economy.

F. THE PROBLEM OF THE MECHANICS OF POWER

One might state in rebuttal to all this that Khrushchev attempted to do something similar in agriculture at the district Party committee level by completely eliminating its economic functions. He made such an attempt—and his political life came to an end. That is true, and it merits special consideration, because apparently no economic reconstruction of the system is possible without a political reconstruction—without a change, if one may put it this way, in the mechanics of power.

The Stalinist mechanics of power is common knowledge. Its decisive instrument is the Plenum of the Party Central Committee—what I call the Soviet parliament. Whereas Stalin's opponents relied on their arguments and eloquence in fighting for a majority in this parliament, Stalin relied on "cadre policy." While his opponents delivered fiery speeches, he installed "his men" as the local satraps, the Soviet prefects who constitute the core of the Plenum. He did not fight for a majority in the parliament; he discovered a means of *molding* a parliamentary majority. When matters reached the point of open conflict, Stalin's men proved deaf to the arguments of his opponents, simply because they were "his men" personally obligated to him for their rise "from the last to the first."

Khrushchev graduated from this school. He knew that the master of the Plenum is master of the country, and he applied the very same technique to his opponents—Malenkov and Molotov. He achieved success, and he believed that it was sufficient for him, just as it had been for Stalin, to attend to the makeup of the Plenum in order to maintain his unshakable authority. But here we encounter the first political paradox of post-Stalin Russia: Khrushchev was overthrown by "his own men." It turned out that the Stalinist mechanics of power is not universal—that it works only under certain conditions. Under precisely what conditions is something that Khrushchev was not destined to find out; therein lay the drama of Khrushchev.

Let us now look at the state of affairs through the eyes of Brezhnev. He went through both schools—Stalin's and Khrushchev's. He learned that the secret of power in the USSR is having "his men" in the Plenum. But Khrushchev's experience taught him that there is a limit to the loyalty even of "his own men"—that they are no longer totally subservient instruments of his power, but constitute a living organism that functions according to its own laws. There is only one thing he does not know: what are these laws? What, consequently, are the limits of his power? What can he venture to do with impunity? Around what corner does Khrushchev's fate await him? That is why his strategy is contradictory: it reflects the unstable balance of forces in the Plenum.

Let us sum up. Both Stalin and Khrushchev were—or considered themselves—masters of the Plenum; therefore, they were fearless; therefore, they were strong leaders. Brezhnev feels like a prisoner of the Plenum; therefore, he is a weak leader. Judge for yourself. He can crush any one of the prefects individually with almost no difficulty, but when they are assembled together they are suddenly transformed into a mysterious, unpredictable, almost mystical force that it is unthinkable to fight against. That is the price that Brezhnev has to pay for preserving the political machine created by Stalin. Stalin still lives through this machine. He has outlived Khrushchev; he may outlive Brezhnev. That is why for the first time in Soviet history a paradoxical situation has arisen (I venture to call this phenomenon a dyarchy) in which the country is being ruled in practice by two Central Committees: the Central Committee apparatus—i.e., six thousand clerks in Staraya Square in Moscow headed by fifteen oligarchs (the Soviet variant of the U.S. Executive branch), and the Central Committee Plenum, dominated by the little Stalins (the Soviet variant of the Legislative branch). It is this "dyarchy" that has paralyzed Brezhnev's political will.[13]

But what might seem to Brezhnev to be an unresolvable antinomy is actually—and on this point my interlocutor and I were in complete agreement—amenable to rational solution. It is simply that the Stalinist mechanics of power, based on the personal relationships between the leader and the members of parliament, can work only given the existence of total terror and a homogeneous social elite. As soon as this terror disappears and the elite becomes differentiated, it becomes apparent that the members of parliament, even though they are the "master's men," personally selected by him, are members of their social groups first and functionaries second.[14] As Khrushchev's experience shows, the interests of the groups they represent are infinitely more important to them than the master's interests.

In short, it is impossible to resolve social conflicts—under post-totalitarian conditions—solely by means of individual changes in the membership of parliament. Khrushchev's mistake was that he attempted to destalinize the system while basing his leadership on the

[13]Here the problem is not only that the Executive and Legislative branches, representing different interest groups, are in constant conflict, but also that, paradoxical as it may sound, the Executive branch has practically no guarantees to protect it against the will of the Legislative branch. That is the *political* manifestation of the social heterogeneity of the post-Stalin elite. It is this social differentiation of the elite that is the principal phenomenon of the post-totalitarian era—a phenomenon of which the elite's political leaders are not yet aware (including Khrushchev and Brezhnev).

[14]In this connection, let us draw attention to a striking phenomenon. Under Stalin the Soviet press was totally unified and seemed to speak with a single voice. Under Khrushchev the public duel between the journals *Novy mir* and *Oktyabr'* (which under Brezhnev has taken a back seat to the duel between *Novy mir* and *Molodaya gvardiya*) became so commonplace that people felt that things had always been that way, that it was natural. It has not occurred to anyone in Russia that this is a manifestation of the heterogeneity of the Soviet elite and of the social struggle stemming from it. But what is most interesting is that even by changing the editors of these journals (Tvardovsky—Kosolapov—Narovchatov in the case of *Novy mir* and Panferov—Kochetov—Anan'yev in the case of *Oktyabr'*) the authorities have been completely unable to bring an end to the duel, because behind each of these journals stands a fully formed interest group. Each new person who sits in the editor's chair—whatever his personal views—has to adapt himself to the supporting interest group. This is another of many forms of evidence that individual personnel changes no longer work.

Stalinist mechanics of power. He did not understand the new alignment of social forces in his parliament, and the Stalinist political machine killed him. A genuine resolution of this paradox probably lies in a leader's basing himself not on *individuals*, but on *interest groups*—or, more precisely, on the representatives of these groups in the parliament. It is apparently a law of post-totalitarian authoritarianism that each interest group must have its political defenders. By basing himself on blocs of these groups, the leader can stabilize his position and free himself from the fear that paralyzes him. Brezhnev is obviously incapable of doing this. My interlocutor, who has associated with such people as Romanov, Dolgikh, and Katushev, was inclined to think that these "young tigers" are capable of understanding the new political realities more quickly than the soon-to-be-extinct "mammoths" from the Stalinist school. If that is so, what has been described above begins to look like something other than a utopian dream. In any case, my interlocutor looked to the future with hope.

Chapter III

THE RIGHT-WING ALTERNATIVE

Up to now we have spoken of phenomena and forces in the present-day USSR that have an interest in one way or another in the country's orientation "toward the West." We have also mentioned the forces that oppose this orientation: the little Stalins, the Soviet military-industrial complex, and the ministers who represent the central economic apparatus. But in the name of what do they oppose it? What alternative can they realistically present in opposition to it? Under what banner can they unite in order to smash the "Western-oriented strategy" of the present leadership and destroy the policy of Detente? If they do not want "coexistence" with capitalism, then what do they want? A world war? World domination? If not that, then what? Does a strategy exist at all that would represent an alternative both to coexistence and to striving for world domination? The answer to this question will be the subject of this third chapter, but before I proceed I want to make an observation about "methodology."

What we shall be dealing with here are not so much material as cultural facts: what could be termed "conceptual reality." People who are accustomed to dealing with accomplished facts do not feel compelled to take into account the incorporeal and ephemeral, what *could* happen—but perhaps that is their loss. Let me offer something in defense of my position on this issue. Let us imagine for a moment that someone in Weimar Germany, when Nazism was still only a "conceptual reality," wrote an article as a warning, asserting that if a serious crisis were to occur, the incorporeal and ephemeral talk about the German people's "historical mission" might evolve into a real political regime that would bring the world much misfortune and perhaps even a global catastrophe. (Essentially the same thing might be asked about Russia of the NEP period, which eventually turned into Stalinist Russia.) What might have been the reaction to a warning of this kind? It would have been possible to dismiss it as an impractical abstraction dealing with things that were politically nonexistent, and in that sense as useless for practical politicians. But it also would have been possible to take it into account in planning strategy. Specifically, one could have tried to plan a strategy of relations—or if you like, detente—with pre-Hitlerite Germany to keep it from ever becoming Hitlerite Germany, provided of course that one admits in principle that foreign policy strategies are closely enough related to domestic political processes that, under certain circumstances, they could have a decisive effect on such processes.

The problem, it seems to me, is that the experience of the transformation of Weimar Germany into Hitlerite Germany was not a strong enough shock for Western politicians to make them feel the urgent need to see the difference between the tactics of day-to-day foreign policy and long-term strategy. The failure to see this difference sometimes turns Secretaries of State into mere firemen who rush to extinguish international conflagrations that have broken out, but who are unable to foresee their occurrence. It seems to me that in principle a long-term strategy cannot be derived from accomplished facts, since its purpose lies precisely in preventing "conceptual realities" from becoming accomplished facts or, on the contrary, in aiding the process leading to their realization. A long-term strategy can be based only on "conceptual realities" such as, for example, the formation of the cultural, social, and political prerequisites for the realization of the "right-wing alternative" in the "Weimar" USSR of today. If and when Russian Nazism becomes an accomplished fact and begins its march to power, it may prove to be too late to influence the process.

I fully realize the unpopularity of this viewpoint, but life in the USSR taught me to reckon with "conceptual reality" no less than with the reality I can grasp with my hands. In any case, I should give advance warning that we shall be dealing with age-old utopias and antediluvian cultural traditions, with novels and samizdat pamphlets that might seem uninteresting to the reader who is too practical-minded.

For the more patient reader, let me remind him that the political culture of a nation may exert a powerful influence on its political reactions and political behavior. And if we can perceive the repetition of a similar pattern of reactions of a nation in the past, it affords us a useful basis for evaluating contemporary reactions. Thus if (as the reader will see in this chapter) a *Neo-Byzantine* orientation of political thought (which consists of a peculiar mix of isolationism and expansionism) appeared in Russia in the 1770's, and again in the 1780's, and then reappeared in the 1860's, 1870's, 1880's, and

1890's, then there should be nothing perplexing about the fact that this orientation has been resurrected in our century as well: in the 1950's, 1960's, and, finally, in the 1970's. The survival of this orientation over several centuries is a fact deserving of our most careful attention. Moreover, as I shall try to demonstrate, this seemingly archaic aspect of Russian national culture corresponds closely to the contemporary political outlook of the "anti-Westerners" within the Soviet elite: both the military-industrial complex and the little Stalins. For precisely this reason it can become the ideological basis for their political strategy after Brezhnev.

A. SERGEY SHARAPOV'S UTOPIA

The novel *Cherez polveka* [After half a century] was published at the very dawning of the twentieth century in the first capital of the tsars—Moscow—which as yet had no presentiment whatsoever of the catastrophe to come in 1917. Its author was Sergey Sharapov, a prominent ideologist of Slavophilism (which had substantially degenerated by that time) and an influential journalist with extremely nationalistic views. "I wanted to give the reader, in the form of a fantasy," he wrote, "a practical compendium of Slavophil dreams and ideals, . . . and to show what could happen if Slavophil views became predominant in society."[1]

How did the adherents of the Russian "extreme right" conceive of their country "after half a century"—i.e., in the middle of the twentieth century? The novel begins with a dialogue. A citizen of the future Russian Empire of the middle twentieth century is talking with a person of like mind from the beginning of the century. The latter naively asks:

> "Is Constantinople really ours?"
> "Yes, it is our fourth capital."
> "Excuse me, but what are the first three?"
> "The government is in Kiev. The second capital is Moscow and the third is St. Petersburg."[2]

[1] S. F. Sharapov, *Cherez polveka* (Moscow, 1901), p. 3.

[2] *Ibid.*, p. 23. In the 1780's a "memoir" entitled *Obshchiye politicheskiye soobrazheniya* [General political considerations] was drawn up in the chancellery of Platon Zubov, then Catherine's favorite. The essence of this "memoir" was that Sweden, Denmark, Prussia, and Austria should cease to exist, while the Russian Empire would acquire *six* capitals: St. Petersburg, Moscow, Astrakhan', Berlin, Vienna, and Constantinople. As can be seen, Sharapov's fantasy was not

For what reason has the government moved from the north to the south, from St. Petersburg to Kiev? It turns out that this was required by the new configuration of the empire's frontiers:

> Persia is now one of our provinces, along with Khiva, Bukhara, and Afghanistan. The western frontier begins at Danzig, includes all of East Prussia as well as Austria and Bohemia and Moravia, passes by Salzburg and Bavaria and drops down to the Adriatic Sea, where it surrounds and includes Trieste. The Russian Empire embraces the Kingdom of Poland and Warsaw, Chervonraya Rus' and L'vov, Bohemia and Vienna, Hungary and Budapest, Serbo-Croatia, Rumania and Bucharest, Bulgaria and Sofia and Adrianople, and Greece and Athens.[3]

The first thing that strikes one about this description of the future Russian Empire is that it does not correspond at all to the Slavophils' traditional conception of the unification of all the Slavic peoples under Russian aegis—a Slavic "Anschluss," so to speak. As is well known, Pushkin had dreamed long before of the time when "the Slavic streams would flow together into a Russian sea"; however, East Prussia, Austria, Afghanistan, Rumania, and Greece are highly questionable "Slavic streams." The orthodox Slavophil from the beginning of the century notes this immediately: "But our dream was that a Union of Slavs would be formed and the Russian Empire would be dissolved in it." The mid-twentieth century citizen replies:

> Listen, that is ridiculous. Look at how immense Russia is and what a small appendage the western Slavs represent. Would it really be just if we, the victors and preeminent among the Slavs, and now in the world as well, were to trim our sails for the sake of some sort of equality with Slavdom?[4]

That means that some other criterion than "Slavic union" has been found for forming the empire. Why has Austria been included but not Bavaria? Why East Prussia and not, for example, Hanover? This is a fundamental question. If we do not answer it, we shall not understand anything about the imperial utopia of Russian nationalism. Therefore, it must be examined in detail.

only not a new idea among the Russian political leadership, but Zubov had gone even further in his thinking about the number of capitals that would be needed by a Russian Byzantium.

[3] *Ibid.*, p. 45.

[4] *Ibid.*, p. 59.

Back in the 1870's one of Sharapov's great predecessors, Fyodor Dostoyevsky, made a prophecy:

> The downfall of your Europe is imminent, and it will be universal, general, and terrible. . . . The anthill has been undermined. . . . What is coming is something that no one even imagines. All these parliamentary doctrines, all the civic theories being professed now, all the accumulated wealth, the banks, the Yids—all of it will be destroyed in an instant and disappear without a trace. . . . All this is quite "close at hand," . . . and I have a premonition that the last line has been written.[5]

The final solution of fateful, millennial questions is "at hand." Apocalyptic presentiments naturally predispose one to prophecies, and Dostoyevsky prophesied. Russia was created by God in order to save the world, and God gave Russia the instrument of salvation—the advanced ideology of Orthodoxy. Russia will save the world because the Russian people are the only people in the world among whom "an enormous majority are Orthodox and live entirely according to the Orthodox idea. . . . In essence, our people have no 'idea' other than this one, and everything else stems from it, and it alone."[6] That is why "when everything collapses, the waves will break only on our shore."

Thus a monopoly on the advanced ideology that is the salvation of all makes Russia alone in the entire world immune to the fatal maladies and evils of the "rotten West," which is being irreversibly drawn into the abyss of a world catastrophe and is dragging a helpless world—excepting Russia—along with it. Russia's mission in world history is not to conquer, subjugate, and gain mastery over this sick world (that would be dangerous, for it could lead to Russia's becoming infected), but rather to save everything from this world that can still be saved.

But Dostoyevsky was not the originator of this messianic conception. It is an ancient and powerful cultural tradition in Russia that first became manifest—that emerged, so to speak, on the stage of history—at least a century and a half ago when the Emperor Alexander, Napoleon's conqueror, rode into Paris on a white steed as the master of half the world. Since that time Russia—in the minds of the nationalist intelligentsia—has been the protagonist of the world

[5]F.M. Dostoyevsky, *Dnevnik pisatelya* [Diary of a writer] (Berlin, 1922), p. 631.

[6]*Ibid.*, p. 665.

drama, while the West has been the antagonist. "Russia's spiritual synthesis versus the rationalism of Europe" is how the issue was posed by the classic Slavophil thinkers in the 1840's. "Holy (Orthodox) Russia versus rotten (Catholic) Europe" was Dostoyevsky's revision thirty years later. "Russia's empire versus the Jews' world empire" was Sharapov's revision of Dostoyevsky after yet another thirty years.

Only the form taken by the advanced ideology changes. In one case it is the "collective consciousness" of Russian culture, in another the Orthodoxy of the Russian people, and in another (after Sharapov's time), socialism. The characteristic that makes the West "rotten" also changes. First it is "parliamentarianism," then "Catholicism," then "Philistinism," and then "the Yids"—the Jewish essence of the West's bourgeois nature, as analyzed by Sharapov. What the Slavophils called the "Europeanization" of Russia was called its "Judaization" by Sharapov, and the "rottenness" of the West was attributed by him to the intrinsic, organic connection between bourgeois thought and the Jews, to the fact that Europe was "already completely under the thumb of the Jews."[7] Sharapov believed, in particular, that war with Germany lay in the future for Russia because that "most recent offspring of the Latin-Germanic world, . . . with no ideals except for those borrowed from the Jews, . . . cannot but hate the new culture, the new light of the world"[8]—i.e., Orthodox Russia, of course. That is why East Prussia had to be a part of the future Russian Empire, but not Bavaria. Two criteria would determine the shape of that empire: one was strategic and the other ideological. Included in the empire would be only those countries that (a) Russia would be able to control directly and (b) whose cultures had not yet been hopelessly contaminated by the Jews.

Thus, Russia had turned out to be the only country in the world that possessed a genuine political alternative to the Jewish plague that had irreversibly vanquished the West—the only country that was capable of erecting a new Great Wall of China, an iron curtain, to halt the Jews' triumphant march, and the only country that, thanks to its authoritarian structure and monopoly on the advanced ideology, was capable of effecting a "final solution to the Jewish question."[9] Therein, according to Sharapov, lay Russia's fundamen-

[7]*Moskovsky sbornik* [Moscow anthology] (Moscow, 1887), p. 26.

[8]*Ibid.*, p. 56.

[9]It is remarkable what similarities exist across a gap of three-quarters of a

tal advantage over Europe, as well as its historical mission. Precisely how the Jewish question was "solved" in the Russia of the future is of course described by the author in detail and with great relish. But suffice it to say that the Jews—the main problem of "the foremost nation in the world" and the "rotten West's" last weapon—were wiped from the face of the Russian earth.

The frontiers of Sharapov's Russian Empire were drawn so as to:

1. Ensure Russia's absolute strategic domination over the West;
2. Guarantee the West's noninterference in the internal affairs of the empire, especially with regard to its methods of solving the Jewish question and the national question in general;
3. Ensure the empire's self-sufficiency, its economic and political autarchy, and its ability to exist independently behind an "iron curtain."

century, between Sharapov's writings and a public lecture given by Soviet ideological official V. Yemel'yanov on February 7, 1973, at Moscow's Central Lecture Hall: "There are four glasses of wine involved in the Jewish Passover ceremony. These glasses symbolize four promises supposedly made to the Jews by God. The first glass symbolizes the exodus from Egypt—that promise has been carried out and the glass is drunk. The Jews did reach Palestine, so the second glass is drunk. The third promise, the gathering of the Jews in Israel after being exiled, has also been carried out. The fourth glass symbolizes the promise to make it unnecessary for the Jews ever to work and to supply them with everything they need. That promise has not been carried out yet, so the fourth glass is not drunk. They are waiting. Who then, comrades, will provide the Jews will all these blessings? You and I, comrades! The Jews are to march to world domination by stepping on the heads of other peoples. It is well known that the Zionists plan to seize power in the entire world by the year 2000. Hitler at his peak held no more than 20 percent of the world economy, and the struggle against him cost our people 20 million lives. World Zionism now controls 80 percent of the world economy. Imagine what the struggle against them will cost us" ("SSSR. Demokraticheskiye al'ternativy" [The USSR: Democratic alternatives] [Achberg, 1976], pp. 216-17). It is very difficult to convey to the foreign reader the electricity that runs from the lecturer to the audience and back again when such words are spoken from an official rostrum. Until then they have felt that they were at opposite poles of the system, cold and estranged, but suddenly they sense their profound inner kinship, suddenly they are in tune with one another. Once again they have one enemy, one common Devil—they are united again. One has to know a Russian's passionate desire to be reconciled with authority, his desire to feel and think in the same way authority feels and thinks, to love and hate the same things, in order to understand how powerful such propaganda is in Russia: *We* stopped fascism and paid with 20 million lives; *we* shall have to pay with 80 million more in order to stop Zionism.

Thus Sharapov manages to combine two seemingly incompatible principles: the *imperial* principle (or, if you will) the principle of limited expansionism), and the *isolationist* principle, which implies an empire hermetically sealed off from the rest of the world. As we can see, Sharapov was not talking about a strategy for world domination, but rather about the adaptation of a Byzantine imperial strategy to the conditions of the twentieth century.[10]

Fate, however, ruled otherwise. Kornilov's coup in August 1917 was unsuccessful, and Kolchak suffered defeat in 1918. The anti-bourgeois and nationalistic "black" alternative prophesied by Sharapov at the beginning of the century went under with them. Victory went to the "red" alternative—also anti-bourgeois, but "internationalist." Orthodoxy was not recognized as the advanced ideology of salvation for all; its place was taken by socialism. Red, not black,

[10]As we have already noted, the roots of Sharapov's utopia go back to a conception that had been thoroughly elaborated by gifted Russian thinkers. In particular, Konstantin Leont'yev—"the greatest, indeed the only great thinker from the conservative camp," according to N. Berdyayev—proposed an essentially similar structure for the Russian Empire of the future. "Russia," Leont'yev wrote, "is not simply a state. Russia . . . is a whole world with its own special life and its own special state system" (K. Leont'yev, *Sobrannyye sochineniya* [Collected works] [Moscow, 1912], Vol. V, p. 380). Russia would be able to realize this "feudal-socialist" scheme only by taking Constantinople, controlling the Mediterranean at least in part, and "assuming the leadership of a new-Eastern state system" (*ibid.*, p. 107) that would stand up against all of Western bourgeois civilization. Like Sharapov, Leont'yev envisioned not world domination, but a world empire. In 1890 Leont'yev predicted the appearance of a "socialist Constantine" whose task would be to "organize socialism" into a great cultural and political force that would stand up against disintegrating Europe, just as his predecessor had organized Christianity into a force that stood up against the disintegration of ancient Rome. But Leont'yev was not the originator of the idea of a new Byzantium that would stand up against the "rotten" West. If historians of Russia look more closely, for instance, at Volume IV of M. Pogodin's collected works, they will find (esp. pp. 4-10) that this idea shows up very clearly in the thinking of the most prominent ideologist of Nicholas's Russia in the 1830's. Or if they were to take a look at the journal *Moskvityanin* (Part I, No. 1, 1831), they would find (on pp. 246ff.) something very similar in S. Shevyrev's famous article "A Russian's View of the Shape of Europe Today." But even half a century before Shevyrev, the secretaries of the then lord of the empire and Prince of Tauris Grigory Potemkin—i.e., Popov and Garnovsky—drew up a plan for creating a new Byzantium. This was a sensation in European newspapers at the time. When a Russian squadron emerged into the Mediterranean Sea in the 1770's, a terrible hue and cry arose in Europe, for Europeans were sure that the Russians' aim was not fighting the Turks, but domination of southern Europe. Thus the "Byzantine" idea has inspired the Russian imperial consciousness for at least 200 years. If the West has forgotten about it, the Russian nationalists have not.

became the official color of the new empire. It seemed that it would be so forever, that Sharapov's Black Hundred dream was consigned to oblivion. The dream was forgotten because it did not become a "fact" that you could grasp with your hands; it was only a "conceptual reality."

B. IVAN SHEVTSOV: REBIRTH OF THE UTOPIA

But "conceptual realities" do not die by themselves. Though the lives of these "realities" are paradoxical and enigmatic, and take forms that at first glance seem to be at variance with their content, they live on—in this case particularly, because both the "anti-Philistine" Russian cultural tradition (which inspired the Slavophils, Dostoyevsky, the Russian populists, Leont'yev, Sharapov, "leftists," and "rightists") and socialism have had a common enemy from the start: the bourgeois West. Therefore, in the minds of the present-day nationalist intelligentsia, Russia and socialism seem to be made for each other—something that Sharapov did not see in his time. The main idea underlying Sharapov's utopia was that an authoritarian Russia possessing an advanced ideology would protect itself, as well as that part of the globe whose security it was in a position to defend, from the plague of world Jewry. Is anything changed in principle by the "fact" that history has made socialism, not Orthodoxy, the advanced ideology? Strictly speaking, is the "red" alternative incompatible with the "black"? All this would be empty speculation if a "black" novel—*Vo imya ottsa i syna* [In the name of the father and the son]—had not been published many decades later (1970) in "red" Moscow. The author was Ivan Shevtsov, who in view of his modest education undoubtedly not only had not read Sharapov's work, but did not even suspect that it existed. Nevertheless, his novel was devoted to a description of what happens as a result of an attempt by world Jewry (Shevtsov uses the term "Zionism," which of course was unknown to Sharapov) to gain control of the last citadel of the "advanced ideology," the bulwark of the anti-Jewish and anti-bourgeois forces in the world today: Russia.[11]

[11]Since Shevtsov's novel is a perfectly legal work published with the censor's blessing, the author sometimes has to make himself understood to his readers more through hints and indirection than by means of frank language. Therefore, it is more difficult to quote from his work than from Sharapov's. I shall provide only a brief synopsis of the novel's essential ideas and political conceptions. The censorship problem is mitigated somewhat by the existence of a nationalist samizdat. Thus at the same time that Shevtsov's legal "black"

First of all, Shevtsov asserts that immediately following Lenin's death Russia was in danger of being taken over by the Zionists . . . in the person of Trotsky. "I remember, and I know very well," says one of Shevtsov's heroes, "what Lev Trotsky was like and what he wanted. He longed to be a dictator. He figured that he could use fuzzy-cheeked youngsters to do away with the communists." Whereas at first Shevtsov's hero merely asserts that "there is a direct and well-traveled path between Zionism and Trotskyism," and that they were brought together by their "desire to rule the world," in literally the very next line he says bluntly: "Trotsky was a Zionist, and his so-called 'party' was a direct offshoot of Zionism."[12] The task assigned to Trotsky by the Zionists was actually a far more drastic one than simply "doing away with the communists." His main objective was to be to eradicate the national consciousness of the Russian people—the only people in the world fighting against Zionism. If he had succeeded, the world would have lost its last chance for salvation. After all, even after Trotskyism had been crushed by Stalin, "the international Zionist syndicate held in its hands 80 percent of all the capital in the entire nonsocialist world," according to a samizdat document that seems to serve as a commentary on the novel. "That is more dreadful than the fascist plague. If they triumph, it means death for everyone."[13] One can scarcely imagine what would have happened had Trotsky been victorious.

Given such a horrendously tragic interpretation of the "red" alternative, some "black" hues inevitably begin to show up in the "red" fabric. The reader is presented with a new picture of the monumental figure of the only leader in the world who dared to throw down an open challenge to the very spirit of world evil—the victor over Trotskyism and savior of Russia: Stalin. If Trotsky was a Zionist and his theory of "world revolution" was an attempt to bring the world under the sway of the "international syndicate," then Stalin was a titan worthy of ancient legends. He is not to blame because his death allowed the nearly liquidated "cosmopolitans" to escape his iron grasp, and because his heirs (especially Khrushchev, whom Shevtsov rather frankly characterizes as a small-time Trotsky

novel was published, the illegal journal *Veche* began to appear in Moscow, and what Shevtsov merely hinted at was frankly explained in the pages of this uncensored journal, as well as in other Russophil samizdat documents. We shall use these documents as a commentary on the novel.

[12] I. Shevtsov, *Vo imya ottsa i syna* (Moskovsky Rabochy Publishing House, 1970), p. 383.

[13] *Novy zhurnal*, No. 118, 1975, p. 223.

in his other novel—*Lyubov' i nenavist'* [Love and hate])—betrayed the cause of the "father of the peoples." True, Khrushchev's Russian colleagues discovered his Zionist leanings in time and stripped him of his power, but alas no new Stalin has been found among them. There has been no one to grasp the Olympic torch from the hands of the titan. There has been no one to smash the policy of "coexistence" with the Zionist-leaning West devised by the cunning Zionist schemers from Khrushchev's circle. (In 1970 Shevtsov knew nothing about such depravity as the policy of Detente, and could not even have imagined that Brezhnev too would tread Khrushchev's fatal path.) As a result the country is experiencing strange, not to say terrible, things (which Shevtsov's novel essentially is devoted to describing). Honest Russian communists are being persecuted while loathsome individuals with Zionist names are scrambling for power. At the behest of the foreign "syndicate," and taking advantage of the pernicious policy of "coexistence," homegrown Zionists[14] are carrying on an extensive campaign to corrupt honest Russian youth in order to make them betray the pure Russian socialist ideals of their fathers.[15]

But what do the Soviet leaders do when they see all these horrible things going on? Nothing. They continue to "coexist" with world Jewry. Essentially they are helping the Jews to "build ideological bridges" without realizing that "coexistence" is a one-way street—a scheme being used by Zionism to win over the hearts and minds of Russian youth. Shevtsov's heroes not only "look with suspicion upon the ideological bridges erected so hastily between cultural figures of the bourgeois West and the socialist countries,"[16] but they also explain to the seemingly blind Soviet leadership that "this alliance is masterminded by international Zionism"[17]—that by

[14]"Zionist-leaning dissidents, with the official support of the U.S. Congress and the governments of other Zionist-dominated Western countries, are attempting by various means to subvert our country from within, in order to pave the way to world domination for the children of Israel" (*ibid.*, p. 224).

[15]One of Shevtsov's heroines recalls that an American journalist told her: "We won't fight Russia. We'll destroy the Russian Communists and the Soviets by peaceful means, using the younger generation, whose upbringing is in our hands. We'll bring them up to think like we do" (Shevtsov, p. 285).

[16]*Ibid.*, p. 378.

[17]*Ibid.*, p. 379. A samizdat document describes the mortal danger posed by "coexistence" even more vividly: "Constant external pressure has led once again to stepped up activity by the Zionist forces in the country. They are in the press and on radio and television. They are in charge of material and technical supply. They worm their way into the circle of friends and advisers of the

sacrificing the principle of sealing off the empire from the rest of the world they are essentially betraying their hapless people to world Jewry. Like Sharapov, Shevtsov perceives that the essence of the West's bourgeois nature (imperialism) is the Jewish plague, which is "more dreadful than the fascist plague." "Do you believe," one of his heroes asks bluntly, "that international Zionism serves American imperialism? I don't believe that. I am convinced that it's the other way around: American imperialism is Zionism's military and economic base, serves Zion's aims and takes care of Zion's needs."[18]

In other words, Shevtsov raises anew Sharapov's "black" banner, which had fallen into the mud after the "internationalist (Trotskyist) red" coup. He needs an iron curtain, not "coexistence." Sealing off the empire completely has become a matter of life and death for Russia, and the "ideological bridges" that Brezhnev (even if involuntarily) is helping Zionism to build are disastrous for it. Shevtsov needs a Stalin, not a Brezhnev. Isolation from America, not cooperation with it, is what he wants: "America reminds me of a bandit who has not run up against a hard fist. But he will, sooner or later he will, and his ugly mug will be so banged up that he'll remember it for a hundred years."[19]

A samizdat document describes the situation even more harshly:

> Just as all Russians, regardless of their views, joined together during the Great Patriotic War to fight the common enemy, so today we must join together to fight against Zionists, unmask and beat all those who are for them and support and encourage all those who are against them. One's attitude toward Zionism is the acid test that reveals patriotism or betrayal. There is no middle ground! Anyone who is not with us is against us. Anyone who is not against Zionism . . . is against Russians, against Slavophils, against *everything decent* on the face of the earth. . . . In the whole chain of problems that confront the Russian people, the key link is the struggle against Zionist domination. By taking hold of this link (and only this one), we will be able to break up the whole chain of problems. If we don't do this, by the year

leaders who have Jewish wives. Essentially, they are once again directing all our country's policies and preparing a new extermination. It is no secret to anyone that the events in Czechoslovakia were instigated by the world Zionist organization through the Goldstueckers" (*Novy zhurnal*, p. 216).

[18] Shevtsov, p. 274.

[19] *Ibid.*

> 2000 the Zionists will physically annihilate the entire Russian people, along with all its problems.[20]

As we can see, Shevtsov and those who think like him are not calling for a global war; it is enough for them merely "to bang up America's mug so that it will remember it for a hundred years." They don't want to be friends, but neither do they want a fight to the death. Let America suffocate by itself in the Zionist gas chamber. Shevtsov's ideal is the same as Sharapov's: isolationist and protective—not world domination, but a neo-Byzantine empire hermetically sealed off from the rest of mankind.

If the Russian people fail to put forward a new great national leader, a new Stalin who will again seal the empire and shut the door on "Zionist domination," the world will be on the verge of catastrophe. Once again, as in Sharapov's time, the authoritarian structure and advanced ideology combined in the unique Russian people are the world's only hope of salvation, for

> communism and Soviet power (*the entire socialist system*) now constitute the only powerful obstacle in the path of Zionism's march to its year 2000. The Russian people are the vanguard of the USSR and consequently of the entire socialist system.[21]

One could describe Shevtsov's novel as an elegy to Stalin if it were not suffused with hope.

C. THE CONCEPTUAL FRAMEWORK OF THE "RIGHT-WING" OPPOSITION

Of course a work approved by the censor with an openly right-wing—i.e., pro-Stalinist—undercurrent was not completely new in Soviet literature after Vsevolod Kochetov's novels *Sekretar' obkoma* [Province committee secretary] and *Chego zhe ty khochesh'?* [What do you want?]. Nevertheless, there is a great deal that makes Shevtsov different from the orthodox Stalinists. Whereas in Kochetov's novels the reader sensed a passionate longing for the "Old Order" and a secret hope that it would be restored, as well as a protestation that the harmonious structure of Soviet power was tilting and almost ready to fall over, new motifs appear in Shevtsov's novel.

Kochetov was free of anti-Semitism and hostile to Great Russian nationalism; he gave no thought to a world Zionist conspiracy. In

[20] *Novy zhurnal*, p. 223. [Emphasis added.]

[21] *Ibid.*, p. 227.

line with tradition, imperialism was to him the embodiment of world evil, but if he said anything about Zionism, it had to do with the "Israeli aggressors." His thinking was, so to speak, a "simple reproduction" (adapted to the realities of the second half of the twentieth century) of the old, pre-revolutionary anti-bourgeois-internationalist "left wing" of Russian extremism that triumphed over the Sharapov-oriented "right wing" in 1917 and became entrenched in Russia under the banner of Marxist socialism.

We should not be misled by the fact that this former "left wing" no longer craved "freedom" but "order," not revolution but reaction—i.e., assumed the garb of the "right wing." In my view, this simply indicates that both "freedom" and "order," both revolution and reaction, have a relative, instrumental significance for the extremist mentality. They are only masks. The underlying basis of extremism is the desire for power. Depending on whether it is striving to gain power or, on the contrary, to stabilize it, extremism changes its masks—from "left wing" to "right wing," or vice versa. The history of Kochetov (and of orthodox Stalinism in general) serves perfectly as experimental confirmation of this point. The *real* division between the two traditional currents of Russian extremism lies in a different plane. The difference is not in their anti-bourgeois nature (in this they are the same) but in their models of world evil and accordingly in their theodicies, in how they vindicate the Good.

Whereas to Kochetov, Zionism is only a weapon of imperialism, to Shevtsov (as we have already seen) it is the other way around. From this difference in their models of evil stem different models of the Good. To Shevtsov, like Sharapov, the essential point is not that the bourgeois world will perish, overwhelmed by its "parliamentary doctrines" and its "Yids"; it is rather Russia's historic mission, the fact that "the waves will break only on our shore." It is precisely the idea that the Russian people are an exceptional, chosen people that sharply divides them from Lenin, for Lenin's concept of the Good is the liberation of the world from the bourgeoisie; therefore, to him Russia is merely an instrument of historical providence. But for Sharapov and Shevtsov, the Good is the salvation of Russia. To them Russia does not play an instrumental role; it is not a means, but an end in itself. Therefore, Lenin's theodicy is aggressive in nature, while Sharapov's is protective. A strategy for world domination ultimately follows from Lenin's theodicy, while a strategy for a neo-Byzantine empire follows from Sharapov's. This is the fundamental difference between Kochetov's Stalinism and that of

Shevtsov. Whereas Kochetov's conception lays stress on what *unites* Lenin and Stalin, Shevtsov's conception emphasizes what *divides* Stalin from Lenin.

D. THE THREE FACES OF STALIN

By analyzing the conceptual framework of the Soviet opposition, we have discovered that the colossal figure of Stalin is not the same to the different Stalinist currents, that in the realm of ideas there are, one might say, several Stalins. Indeed, in turns out that Stalin, as the Lord God, is present in at least three hypostases in the opposition consciousness today. First, there is Stalin the Father, so to speak—leader of the industrialization of backward Russia and accordingly creator of the Russian working class. It is this Stalin who predominates in the mind of Kochetov, for whom the working class is the principal subject of literary works, the alpha and omega of all wisdom in life. This Stalin was the leader of world communism and a pillar of the "Old Order." Second, there is a Stalin—Stalin the Son we shall call him—who breathed new life into Russian nationalism and embarked on a fight to the death against Zionism. This Stalin, who restored Russia's traditional imperial image, is completely alien to Kochetov, but predominates in the mind of Shevtsov. Finally, there is Stalin—if one may put it this way—as the Holy Spirit. It should not be forgotten that the USSR Constitution now in effect, whose proper implementation is demanded by the great bulk of the dissident movement, was called the "Stalin Constitution" for two decades. In the minds of most of the Russian people, who consider it "the most democratic constitution in the world," a sort of Magna Carta of socialism, its author was Stalin. The paradoxical circumstance that the dissident movement, which is resolutely anti-Stalinist in nature, is nonetheless devoting all its energies to fighting for the implementation of the Stalin Constitution testifies to the fact that Stalin is also present in their doctrine at least as the "Holy Spirit."

Thus the three images of Stalin are essentially the points of departure for practically all the opposition currents in the USSR. If one does not distinguish among them, the "conceptual reality" of the present-day USSR will appear to be only a chaotic conglomeration of stillborn utopias rather than a vigorous battle among different political programs for the country's transformation. One of these programs is ultimately destined to triumph and thereby be transformed from an ephemeral "conceptual reality" into a formidable political reality.

E. REBIRTH OF AN OLD DEVIL

It is generally assumed that an extraordinary structure like the USSR that has a single ideology and is medieval in nature can exist only on the basis of a clear conception of some global enemy—of what could be termed the "Devil" of the conceptual framework. Whether the ideology that gives this structure its basis for existence is considered "advanced" or "traditional" depends on how this Devil is defined. In 1901 Sharapov had his Devil, and Lenin had *his*; they seemed to be completely irreconcilable. From this standpoint, the paradox of Soviet history is how it came about that Lenin's Devil was gradually transformed into Sharapov's. In other words, how did a "conceptual reality" that had been buried and forgotten begin to gain mastery over a triumphant political reality? What could have been the genesis of this transformation? How did the "black" alternative evolve from the "red" one? Stalin's experience, it seems to me, can serve to some extent as a model of this process. We shall be attempting only a hypothetical reconstruction, but as yet we have no other instruments of analysis in this sensitive area.

Stalin inherited his original Devil from Lenin, of course. It was the innocent and universal bourgeois Devil, unburdened by any national syndromes and prejudices. This was a Devil from whom one could liberate the world with the help of the advanced ideology of socialism, with its immaculate faith in the power of world proletarian solidarity to save the world and its belief that proletarians have no homeland.

For some reason proletarian solidarity did not make the Polish workers turn their bayonets against the Polish bourgeoisie in 1920. There was the same proletarian failure in all three Baltic republics. The pertinacity of the Finnish working class in the war of 1940 further confirmed the ineffectiveness of Lenin's Devil. It was found that the proletariat does have a homeland, and every time it has to choose between proletarian solidarity and its homeland, it stubbornly prefers the latter. The heaviest blow dealt to Lenin's Devil was the dashing of the hope that the German proletariat would behave differently when the homeland of social democracy clashed with the homeland of socialism. (This hope was extremely widespread in Russia even as late as 1941.) But the German working class proved to be dedicated to the "national idea" not one particle less than the German bourgeoisie. That is probably why Stalin, when he addressed the people on July 3, 1941, used the Orthodox greeting "brothers and sisters" rather than the proletarian "comrades," and why the war was proclaimed the Patriotic War in a country formally ruled by the dictatorship of a proletariat without a homeland. Lenin's Devil did not survive the test of experimental verification.

That moment of great national crisis was when Stalin came to believe once and for all in Sharapov's old, tried and true Devil, which had withstood the experimental test of Nazism. But in order to transform the new Devil into the old one, it was not enough simply to supplement socialism with historic national symbols or to resurrect the traditional slogan "autocracy, Orthodoxy, and nationality." (All that had existed under the tsar in 1901, and it did not suit Sharapov; it was from that that he fled to his utopia.) The most important element was still lacking: the Devil had to be something against whom the people would be ready to fight to their deaths, as they were in 1917. Not an official Devil but, so to speak, a non-Party Devil for the masses, for the nation. As the campaign against "rootless cosmopolitans" and the legal proceedings against the "murderers in white smocks" show, Stalin found this Devil.

Stalin was not an expert in Russian nationalist thought; he found this Devil by himself. He found it by following his political intuition and using his knowledge of the culture of the people he ruled for a quarter of a century. This gives his choice enormous significance. Even "after half a century" of proletarian dictatorship in Russia, no more effective Devil could be found than the Jews. During the revolution of 1905 the Bolsheviks battled the Black Hundreds, Sharapov's followers, those who were fighting for the "black" alternative, and they had no more contemptible enemy than the "League of the Russian People." But "after half a century" the Bolsheviks began to turn into the Black Hundreds, and the Communist Party into the heir of the "League of the Russian People."

F. UNCOMPLETED TRANSFORMATION

The definition of Stalin's last invention (and therefore Shevtsov's ideological conception as well) is now obvious. It is socialism supplemented by nationalism, by faith in the Russian nation's being the chosen people (not the world proletariat, but the Russian people!) and in its historic mission of establishing a "New Order." Hitler was defeated when he tried to accomplish a similar task, but what does that prove—other than the erroneousness of a strategy of world domination and the historic inferiority of the German people, other than that they are not the chosen people, the Messiah?

Not world domination, but a neo-Byzantine empire. Not the

German people, but the Russian people. With this historical correction, the Devil that misfired in Hitler's hands will blaze away for Stalin.

But Stalin died before he could carry out his titanic scheme. The idea of the new Devil did not become a real force; the transformation of the Party into the "League of the Russian People" was not completed; the Jewish question in Russia was not solved once and for all. The old ruling core of the Politburo, irrevocably warped by archaic Marxist prejudices and therefore unprepared for such a sharp change in policy, was not removed. Finally, a strategy for building the empire was not worked out.

G. A NEW BYZANTIUM

Until now we have tended to talk about the domestic political side of the transformation of the "red" alternative into the "black," but what is of even greater interest, of course, is the foreign policy aspect. In order to reconstruct the foreign policy transformation, we shall have to start at the beginning again, with the universal concept of "world revolution" that inspired Lenin. After capitalism regained its stability in the 1920's, which was catastrophic for this concept, a dispute arose in the Party regarding strategy. This strategy dispute was the real cause of the factional struggle. The inflexible Marxists of the opposition, who had no flair for strategy, insisted on the bankrupt concept of "world revolution." Stalin's cadres countered with the concept of "building socialism in one country" and coexistence with capitalism. They triumphed in alliance with the Bukharinites, who sincerely believed in this new strategy, in which they saw essentially a plan for rational state construction. The Bukharinites made a mistake, however. In Stalin's mind this new strategy had an entirely different meaning, judging by the fact that after he had crushed the Trotskyists, he adopted a Trotskyist or even super-Trotskyist domestic political platform.

Stalin's reasoning may have been simple. The West is doomed; its downfall is a matter of time and one more good big war. The First World War had simply not been enough to destroy it once and for all. A second war will be required, in which the capitalists will destroy each other. The only thing that is required of socialism is to be ready for the Day of Judgment that awaits capitalism. If that means it is necessary to make the peasants serfs, "attach" the workers to the factories, institute total terror and turn the country into a concentration camp with "the most democratic constitution in the world"—

that is not too high a price to pay for becoming master of the world. Thus Stalin's strategic goal became not rational state construction, as it was for Bukharin; not world revolution, as it was for Trotsky; and not even "building socialism in one country," as it was for Kirov; but something entirely different—a dawning dream of *world domination*. That is why Trotsky and Bukharin and Kirov had to be destroyed. Not just one country, but the world was at stake now.

The war came. But along with victory it brought the collapse of Stalin's strategy, for there was no Day of Judgment. After the war the USSR turned out to be as far from world domination as it had been before. Stalin is generally thought of as the great victor in the "battle of nations," but it seems to me he was defeated in his effort to achieve his main objective—the only one that really mattered to him. His great worldwide dream was shattered. It became clear that he would never be the emperor of a Third Rome that would unite East and West, and domination over Poland or Rumania could never take the place of the Third Rome for him. Something else, something even worse, also became clear to the "father of the peoples"—the dream itself, the very idea of socialist world domination, was unrealizable.

The demise of this dream and the strategy for achieving it can be portrayed graphically. If one imagines the socialist world as a kind of solar system, then the so-called union republics are the planets revolving around the nucleus—Russia—in the first orbit. In the second orbit are satellites with more autonomy, such as Poland, Bulgaria, etc. In the third orbit are satellites with even more autonomy, such as Yugoslavia and Rumania. If one examines closely what the Ukrainian nationalists are seeking, for example, it turns out that what they want initially is something like Poland's status—i.e., a shift to the second orbit. What did Czechoslovakia want in 1968? Merely the status of Yugoslavia—i.e., a shift to the third orbit. As is shown by the experience of Rumania, which deviated from the orthodox axis not "to the left" but "to the right" and jumped from the second orbit to the third before the eyes of an astonished Europe, this is by no means a hopeless dream. Czechoslovakia's mistake was not that it wanted to make this jump, but that it did not take into account the laws governing such movement—namely, that in the socialist system moving outward to the next orbit is, so to speak, a street on which traffic must keep to the right and that, in drivers' parlance, passing is allowed only on the right.[22]

[22]Here the West is confronted with a knotty moral and political problem. It must be cognizant to some extent of what it is striving most for: the democra-

That is not what interests us right now; instead, it is the fact of the orbital rather than uniform nature of the socialist empire. In other words, expansion of the socialist world directly controlled by orders from a single center, from Moscow, which was the aim of Stalin's strategy, led to the opposite result: the intensification of centrifugal tendencies destructive of the system. The difference between the orbits in the system lies in the extent to which the satellites can be directly controlled. From this standpoint, the fact that it proved impossible to make Poland, Bulgaria, and Hungary constituent parts of the USSR (as had been done only five years before in the cases of Lithuania, Latvia, and Estonia) was an ominous sign to Stalin. The proletarians of all countries had again failed to show a desire to unite. On the contrary, it turned out that from the very beginning all the satellites were subject to a centrifugal pull of enormous strength that inevitably drew them outward toward the next orbit—i.e., toward a reduction in the extent to which they could be directly controlled. When Yugoslavia willfully jumped to the second orbit in 1947, and Mao took power in Peking, it must have become clear to Stalin that the socialist system had not only revealed latent tendencies toward self-destruction, but could even break up altogether if one more orbit were to come into existence. As we now know, that is what happened. The formation of a fourth orbit led after a few years to the world's becoming witness to a mortal confrontation between the two major socialist powers.

But if it had been *proven* that the strategy of socialist world domination was unrealizable, then what remained? What could the alternative be? What could be the new strategy that would make it possible to maintain the basic parameters of the system—its imperial character, its militarist nature, its GULAG Archipelago—and at the same time would protect it from the rise of fatal intra-socialist antagonisms? How could a Byzantine empire, rigidly and directly controlled from a single center, still be created in the middle of the twentieth century?

It seems to me that the only answer was the imperial-isolationist strategy. In other words, the need was to create a special, distinctly Russian political universe hermetically sealed off from the rest of the world, a universe with anti-bourgeois laws, with a regime of terror, and as Leont'yev predicted, with a "feudal-socialist" state organiza-

tization of Eastern Europe or the weakening of East European ties with the USSR? As history has shown (not only in the case of Rumania, but also in China, North Korea, Albania, and Vietnam), these two aims by no means always coincide.

tion. This meant creating the "new Eastern civilization" dreamed of by Leont'yev in the 1880's, the "Great Russian Empire" advocated by Sharapov at the beginning of the century. It meant creating a new Byzantium.

H. DEFENSE OF THE HYPOTHESIS

What can be said in defense of this hypothesis? First of all, the imperial-isolationist strategy was the *only* alternative to both the unrealizable strategy of socialist world domination and the strategy of rational state construction, which presupposed a fundamental economic and political reconstruction of the system. It is obvious that Stalin did not intend to embark on such a reconstruction of a new NEP. (In any case, there is absolutely no indication that he did.) To me it is no less obvious, in light of everything set forth above, that Stalin was not preparing for a final assault on world capitalism.

Why then—and this is my second point in defense of the hypothesis—did Stalin keep under arms an army of many millions that was considerably larger than the present-day army? Why was he preparing to test the hydrogen bomb in 1953?

Third, why was Stalin preparing for the "final solution" of the Jewish question in Russia?

Fourth, why was Stalin rapidly reviving the tsarist-imperial symbols? (Even Alexander III and Nicholas I did not make Russia squeeze itself into uniforms, sport epaulets, and rattle its sabers as much as Stalin did.)

Fifth, why was Stalin preparing for a new purge of the elite and for the liquidation of his most loyal comrades-in-arms, with whom he had crushed all opposition? Let us recall that he carried out a similar purge in the late 1930's because of a change in strategy he was preparing to carry out. Isn't it logical to assume that a new change in strategy was in the works in the early 1950's, and that it was necessary to wipe out potential opposition to it?

It seems to me that the answer to all these questions is given at the end of the preceding section (pp. 62-63).

I. THE STRUCTURE OF THE "NEW ORDER"

The internal organization of the new Byzantium, stretching from Canton to Berlin, from the South China Sea to the Adriatic (i.e., in the west roughly to the frontiers drawn by Sharapov, and in Asia to the frontiers to which the socialist soldier had succeeded in marching), would have been "feudal socialism." In other words, it would have been what already existed in the USSR—a combination of slave and serf labor, a rigidly centralized administration (in time modernized through automation and computerization), terror, ideological control, and an iron curtain. The changes would have been purely quantitative: the number of republics in the USSR would have increased, let us say, from sixteen to thirty, so as to include the Chinese, Korean, Serbian, Croatian, Polish, Montenegrin, and other republics. Qualitative changes would have occurred mainly in the ideological sphere: the Russian people would have been officially recognized as "first among equals"; its material standard of living would have been sharply raised by extorting resources from the national republics, both old and new; not only its national history, but also its historic church would have been restored to it; the Orthodox Church would have taken part in the life of society on roughly the same basis as in the old tsarist empire; the source of the Russian people's spiritual greatness—its historic mission of standing up against the "rotten West"—would have been restored to it; the official aim of the empire would have become a struggle not simply against imperialism, but against "imperialism in the service of Zionism," whose waves would have broken, as Dostoyevsky had it, "on our shore"; and finally, if there were spontaneous uprisings in the capitalist world against "Jewish domination," the ten- or twenty-million man Russo-Sino-German army would have immediately extended its fraternal assistance to the revolutionary nation (Vietnam, say, or Italy), making it the thirty-first or thirty-second republic of the union of fraternal peoples, a union completely free of both Jewish domination and capitalist exploitation.

That is why Stalin needed a ten-million man army and the hydrogen bomb: so that the Zionist West would not dare to interfere in the organization of the new Byzantium, so that the curtain separating it from the outside world would remain an iron curtain, so that the military-industrial complex would continue to dominate the Soviet-Byzantine economy, and so that no national uprisings would take place in the new empire—or if they did, they would be drowned in blood so that no one beyond the iron curtain would hear anything about them. If sixty million Germans—with the help of Nazi Quislings—could control all of Europe, then why couldn't one hundred million Russians—with the help of socialist Quislings—control the new Russian Empire?

Of course, it may be objected that this has an Orwellian ring to it, but I would like to be told why it was impossible. And why *will it be* impossible if the new Russian "right" finds its Stalin—someone who will give the country what its present leaders, who have become enmeshed in a hodgepodge of doctrinairism and pragmatism, cannot give it?

J. ON THE EVE OF A NEW ASSAULT

Up to this point I have tried to show (a) that the "conceptual reality" of the "right-wing" extremist alternative is deeply embedded in the Russian national consciousness; (b) that at times of acute national crisis the "right wing" generally mounts an assault against the existing strategy in an effort to achieve political self-realization; (c) that such assaults took place not only in 1905 and 1917, but also in 1953; and (d) that the political, conceptual, and social prerequisites for a new assault are approaching fulfillment in the Weimar USSR of today.

In order to prove this last and most important point, I could refer to the fact that Shevtsov's "black" novels would not have been passed by the censor under any circumstances if not for the personal intervention of D. Polyansky, then a member of the Politburo, who was one of the unsuccessful candidates for the role of the new Stalin and came very close to supplanting Kosygin in 1970. The point of this reference is to establish the fact that at the very "apex" of the Soviet leadership a group already existed that was prepared to adopt the Nazi program, and that this group held powerful positions in the mass media and was not afraid of making its program public both in Shevtsov's novels and in a series of articles in the journal *Molodaya gvardiya* in 1968-70. Polyansky's star has set, but who can know when and under what circumstances the star of Solomentsev, for example, will reach its zenith?

I could also refer to a document that I consider of the utmost importance, since it gives one an idea of the current expectations of young nationalists. At a time when the leader of the democratic dissident movement, Andrey Sakharov, has frankly declared that he is pessimistic and skeptical about the regime's becoming more liberal,[23] the leader of the nationalistic dissident movement, G. Shimanov (according to rumor the author of the semi-fascist manifesto *The Nation Speaks*), has nothing but the highest hopes. In particular, he writes in the samizdat document *An Open Letter to the Patriarch*:

[23] A. Sakharov, *V bor'be za mir* [In the struggle for peace] (Posev Publishers, 1973), p. 117.

> There can be no doubt that eliminating the destructive elements from Soviet legislation and its application will have a morally salutary effect on Soviet society, for that will link it with the thousand-year-old moral roots of Russia, strengthen Soviet power itself and do away with the environment in which anti-Soviet sentiments can grow, and it will also attract millions of conscious patriots to the side of a harmonized Soviet state. There are substantial grounds for hoping that the Soviet leaders will understand this in the near future and move in the direction of their own interests.[24]

This was written on July 15, 1976. In contrast to Sakharov, Shimanov has considerable opportunity to find out what the Soviet leaders "will understand in the very near future." After all, along with him and his comrades, the "Society for the Preservation of Monuments of History and Ancient Times" numbers among its members such people as Vice-Chairman of the RSFSR Council of Ministers Kochemasov and Marshal Chuykov (whom, incidentally, Shevtsov portrayed very sympathetically in his novel)—i.e., people who are fairly well acquainted with the plans or intentions, or at least the hopes, of some of the Soviet leaders.

In addition, there are other, more objective factors:

1. Which of the political factions involved in one way or another in the country's leadership could have an interest in such a change in strategy? Let us direct our attention first to the ambiguous position of the military and the military-industrial complex in an era of Detente and unceasing attempts by the leadership to breach their economic hegemony. It is obvious that any economic reform, any real improvement in relations with the West, any arms reduction constitutes a threat to this hegemony. On the other hand, a call for a global war in an era of nuclear weapons would be absurd. What then remains for this powerful group other than the middle path of empire, other than the "right-wing" alternative? Only this alternative would make it possible both to avoid global war and to justify a further arms buildup and the maintenance of the economic dictatorship of the military-industrial complex. It is clear that "establishing order" in China or the Balkans and "maintaining order" in newly annxed "union" republics would constitute not just a police operation, but a strategic military task of tremendous complexity that might take many decades to accomplish. In other words, the "right-wing" alternative is essentially the ideal solution to all the problems of this segment of society. Whereas Detente makes the position of

[24] *Novoye russkoye slovo*, October 2, 1976.

the military-industrial complex in society ambiguous, the imperial strategy makes its role ideologically and politically meaningful to the highest degree. Perhaps that is why Shevtsov is so sympathetic toward Marshal Chuykov, and Marshal Chuykov takes such an interest in "monuments of history."

Thus we see clearly one group whose interests objectively coincide with the "right-wing" alternative. A second group is the "little Stalins," the Soviet prefects. Their main competitors today are the managers because the latter lay claim to economic independence and consequently threaten to deprive the prefects of their organizational function in the economy, which serves to justify their political domination of society. In the atmosphere of economic reform created by the present leaders, this threat is becoming a continuing one. The fact that the prefects have managed to fend it off up to now offers them no guarantees for the future, which may bring stronger and more consistent leaders. There is no room for them in a healthy and rationally organized economy, and their continued existence would be uncertain. The imperial strategy, on the other hand, would provide entirely different opportunities for "reconstructing the economy" (by means of the forcible exaction of resources from foreigners and national minorities). This strategy could practically eliminate competition from the managers by restoring to the economic structure its "simple" Stalinist harmony and the combination of ministerial vertical authority and the prefects' horizontal authority.

The same line of argument is applicable to the central economic apparatus and the ministers. The imperial strategy would give them a chance to suppress completely all tendencies toward the decentralization of the economy.

Today these three factions possess an absolute majority in the Soviet parliament, the Party Central Committee. This means that in order to make the new strategy a reality not even the "destruction of the old state machine" will be required, but only a serious social, economic, or military crisis that will make it perfectly clear that there no longer exists any other alternative that will enable them to maintain their political domination of society, and that the contradictory strategy of the present Weimar leadership, which has attempted to use Detente as a substitute for reconstructing the country's economy, has outlived its usefulness. To realize the new strategy will require a strong *leader* capable of joining these three heterogeneous factions into a unified political force, a unified *program* for shifting to the new strategy that takes into account the interests of all the groups mentioned, and a favorable spiritual *atmosphere* in society—a prevailing attitude of mind that would facilitate the transition.

That is how matters stand with regard to the fulfillment of the *political* prerequisites for the "right-wing" alternative.

2. Turning to the current public *atmosphere* (or to the formation of the *conceptual* prerequisites for the "right-wing" alternative), we observe that in the ideological vacuum that has formed as a result of the collapse of Marxist stereotypes in the minds of thinking "young Russia," new spiritual leaders have emerged—namely, the most brilliant prophets of Russian messianism: Dostoyevsky and Berdyayev. Even believers, of whom there are now many as a result of the Orthodox Renaissance that has gripped the young Russian intelligentsia, invoke the names of Berdyayev and Dostoyevsky more often than those of Jesus and the holy apostles. It is obvious that the influence of these new spiritual leaders is anti-Western, anti-bourgeois, and both Orthodox and socialist. Berdyayev is playing much the same role in Russia today that Marx played in the 1890's. At that time it seemed to the tsarist police that the general enthusiasm for Marxism was merely an academic phenomenon. (The tsarist police assessed "conceptual realities" in much the same spirit as some present-day political observers.) But the police were mistaken. From the ranks of these young students came hundreds and thousands of fiery advocates of a new idea, the future organizational cadres of a movement that accomplished what seemed inconceivable by smashing a mighty, petrified empire that had stood for three hundred years.

The protest of nationalistic "young Russia" is also based on a number of objective factors: (a) the dictatorship of ignorant leaders (their ignorance is as galling in this context as their dictatorship) is perceived by the young Russian intelligentsia as a national humiliation, as a new Tatar yoke, and thus feeds the fatal national inferiority complex; (b) in the minds of the young, the Russian people are already facing a demographic catastrophe;[25] (c) the Russian countryside—traditional source of the nation's physical and psychological health—is rapidly degenerating and decaying;[26] (d) the cultural level

[25]See, for example, the "Letter to the Editors" of the journal *Vestnik RSKhD* [Bulletin of the Russian Student Christian Movement] from V. Osipov, former editor of the journal *Veche*: "Our so-called 'nationalism' . . . is a manifestation of the instinct of self-preservation on the part of a *vanishing* nation. . . . Our people are vanishing quantitatively. . . . I believe that even the problem of human rights in the USSR is less important at this juncture in history than the problem of the *dying* Russian nation" (*Vestnik RSKhD*, No. 106, p. 295; emphases added).

[26]"One may say in all seriousness that the destruction of the Russian village

of the Russian people, who have been forcibly deprived of their traditional historic aims and their age-old religion, has declined to a critical point.[27]

In the minds of the young nationalists there is only one solution to all this. As V. Osipov writes: "I am absolutely convinced that there is no way out of the moral and cultural impasse in which Russia finds itself other than reliance on Russian national consciousness."[28] At the same time these young people, while in complete agreement with Berdyayev's precepts, are not at all opposed to socialism. What is more, they are convinced that it is precisely Soviet power that offers the basis for achieving a genuine national and religious renaissance.[29] Is it surprising that this outlook, which links nationalism and socialism, has given rise to the initially paradoxical-sounding slogan of "combining Leninism and Orthodoxy" as a panacea that will bring total salvation?[30] Can this slogan be called anything but national-socialist?

. . . is a refined but reliable means of destroying this nation" (*Vol'noye slovo* [An unfettered statement] [Posev Publishers, 1975], p. 31).

[27]"We now observe among the Russian people an unbridled rampage of Philistinism, self-seeking, egoism, and indifference to the public interest. The honest segment of Russian society is growing smaller and smaller in number, in particular because people succumb to the temptation of an easy life that emanates from 'certain representatives' of certain 'national minorities' [a euphemism for Jews—A. Yanov]. The pocketbook and the bottle threaten to swallow up all the other interests of Russians" (*ibid.*, p. 32).

[28]Osipov continues: "I myself am a believer. In the final analysis, I prefer Christ and his teachings to nationalism. But I know the Russian soul today: at present the national element is more alive and more distinct than the religious element. . . . For the time being it is the only reliable bridge to moral and cultural, to biological salvation!" (*Vestnik RSKhD*, No. 106, p. 295).

[29]"A Soviet social and political system based on national principles and the genuine observance of the USSR Constitution is perfectly acceptable to us," says Osipov (*ibid.*, p. 303). Shimanov is even more direct: "Without the Soviet system, with its latent religious nature and its potential opportunities, Orthodoxy in our history will not be brought to fruition socially" (*Novoye russkoye slovo*). The following appears in a samizdat document: "Soviet power, by replacing the autocracy, accomplished what was most important—it deprived the Zionists in our country of the right to private ownership of the instruments and means of production. Perhaps some people are sick of hearing about that, but if it had been otherwise the year 2000 would have come for the children of Israel long ago. . . . The slogan of granting freedoms really means that Solzhenitsyn and Sakharov want to give back to the Zionists the right they lost in 1917" (*Novy zhurnal*, No. 118, p. 224).

[30]This slogan was advanced as the logical conclusion of a series of articles about Russian Slavophilism written by M. Antonov and published in the first

That is how the *conceptual* prerequisites for the "right-wing" alternative are being fulfilled in the Russia of today, as it stands at the crossroads.

3. As for the *social* prerequisites, it may be said that they are already fully achieved. This is a result of the gigantic, historically unprecedented migration from the Russian countryside, which has devastated northeastern Russia, the cradle of the nation, and is now devastating Siberia. An enormous, psychologically unstable mass of recent migrants from the countryside has formed in the rapidly growing cities, people who think in terms of peasant stereotypes and suffer from "migration culture shock."[31] These urban masses have traditionally been infected with nationalistic prejudices, and experience has shown that it is easy to convince them of the justice of the regime's imperial undertakings,[32] as well as to use them to combat the dissident movement. In this connection, it is sufficient to call attention to the role of the so-called "volunteer militia aides," who break up dissident demonstrations[33] and religious gather-

three issues of *Veche*. This viewpoint obviously reflects the position of the editors because in the letter from Osipov that has been cited, along with a statement of approval for the "Soviet socialist system," appears the following: "I am not a Marxist, and I cannot see the soul of Russia as Marxist" [i.e., as Jewish-German—A. Yanov] (*Vestnik RSKhD*, No. 106, p. 294).

[31]When in my sociological essays on migration published in *Literaturnaya gazeta* in 1966, I put forward the hypothesis that migration might be the leading cause of crime among young people in the cities, it was immediately supported by legal theoreticians who had specially researched the social makeup of "violators of the criminal code" in Moscow. In general, the letters that I received after the publication of these essays showed that specialists in the most diverse fields of knowledge saw the key to many negative phenomena in present-day Soviet society in the phenomenon of "migration culture shock" I had suggested. For example, according to information from medical researchers who study the causes of sexual pathology, about 75 percent of the urban males suffering from impotence are recent migrants from the countryside. Thus "migration culture shock" (I do not know how well known this Soviet phenomenon is in the American literature) has proved to be one of the most serious afflictions of the Soviet urban population, affecting not only the way migrants behave, but also the very biological foundations of their personalities.

[32]According to a Russian proverb: "No matter how much you feed a wolf, he always looks to the forest" (i.e., he will show no gratitude)—that was the general reaction among the urban lower strata to the Prague Spring of 1968.

[33]See N. Gorbanevskaya's book *Polden* [Red Square at noon]. When the seven protesters against the invasion of Czechoslovakia went out into Red Square, the first words spoken by the volunteer militia aides as they attacked them were: "Mates, it's all the Yids' doing!"

ings,[34] provide the main contingent of spectators at today's political trials, and willingly beat up anyone indicated by the authorities; they are especially willing to beat up Jews.[35] Their openness to chauvinist ideas is obvious.[36] The "internal enemy" is the Jews and the intellectuals (who are one and the same to them), while the "external enemy" is all non-Russian peoples, whose main aim, as they see it, is to suck the lifeblood from Russia. The slogan "Steal what has been stolen!" would undoubtedly evoke an effective and ardently patriotic response in their hearts.[37] They would go to their deaths for it, as their grandfathers went in 1917. Essentially the "volunteer militia aides" today are the prototypes of the traditional "Black Hundreds." In their eyes the West is still the same as it was in Sharapov's time—the Sodom and Gomorrah of Zionism.[38]

[34]See Solzhenitsyn's description of this unruly mob of urban plebeians in his story "Paskhal'ny krestny khod" [The Easter procession] (*Vestnik RSKhD*, No. 91).

[35]The most recent mass beating of Jewish activists in Moscow (in October 1976) confirms anew this unhappy conclusion.

[36]It is so obvious that it is utilized by the KGB, which has tried to blackmail Sakharov in the name of the "Russian Christian Party." See the statements by Sakharov and his son-in-law Yankelevich in the journal *Kontinent*, No. 9, 1976.

[37]In this case, "what has been stolen" would mean everything possessed by the non-Russian peoples of the socialist commonwealth, for as the volunteer militia aides understand it, all this "has been stolen" by them from the Russians, regardless of whether the people are the Jews, the Georgians, the Czechs, the Chinese, or the Poles. In this regard, the following appears in a samizdat document: "On October 20, 1972, *Literaturnaya gazeta* printed this in an article: 'In order to put an end to the relative backwardness of the national republics more quickly, the Communist Party and the Soviet government have developed their economics at faster rates. For example, whereas by 1940 the country's production had increased 1,200 percent, in the national republics growth was far greater: 1,900 percent in Kazakhstan, 15,200 percent in Kirgizia, and 32,300 percent in Tadzhikistan.' . . . Where did these resources come from? Bread was torn from the mouths of Russians and given to others. While Georgia now has excellent roads and electricity and its people live in plenty, in the native Russian northern provinces there are no good roads and the only people left in the villages are old people who are practically beggars; indeed, there are many villages that no longer exist at all" (*Novy zhurnal*, No. 118, p. 213).

[38]The following appears in a samizdat document: "Everything in the West belongs to rich Jews now. First, political power. All ten of President Nixon's advisers are prominent Zionists. He doesn't dare to take a single step without the Jew Kissinger. Goldberg at the UN, Linkovich in South Africa, Abraham Fortas on the Supreme Court, Javits in the Senate, etc. They contrive the comedy of 'democratic elections.' They put the Irish Kennedys out of the way. Pompidou, the President of France, once worked for the House of Rothschild.

Is it possible to imagine a situation in which all these heterogeneous forces would work together for the purpose of united political action? Russian history, even comparatively recently, has known combinations even less likely. Could one have imagined that the enormous peasant masses, who hungered for a division of the landowners' estates into property, would join together in a struggle against the regime with a group of Marxist dogmatists who were fanatical in their rejection of property? However, this happened in 1917—and that explosive mixture, a kind of social nuclear energy, demonstrated incredible power. Could one have imagined that the *bureaucratic* machine would join together with the *anarchic* lumpenpeasantry to destroy the economically enterprising segment of the peasantry? However, this happened in 1929—and determined the country's fate for the next half-century.

It is important to remember two things about these historical "combinations." First, in both cases the same slogan—"Steal what has been stolen!"—served as the detonator for setting off these "social bombs." Second, the role played by the village mob in the past is played in today's urbanized Russia by the lower strata of the cities, a tremendous mass of unskilled manpower, people who have lost their traditional peasant morality and so far have found no other. These are the people of whom Solzhenitsyn said: "They will roll over some time—and we shall all be crushed!"

In this regard, it is dangerous that the authorities themselves, in their efforts to counter the devastating criticism from the dissident movement and "subversive" foreign radio broadcasts, are appealing too often and too easily to the basest instincts of these masses—the instincts that lead them to commit pogroms. It is dangerous that the authorities are already unable to find any ideological defense against their opponents other than such appeals, which aggravate the moral crisis among this explosive urban mass. They do not understand that they themselves can be crushed by the mob if it finds leaders (who, as we have seen, are already in the starting gates).

It only remains for me to say that—in my opinion—a crisis in which this "conceptual reality" of the "right-wing" alternative could

The members of all the Western governments are either Jews or Masons (the Masons are a secret political organization . . . that unquestioningly does the bidding of the Sanhedrin, the Jewish leadership). . . .

"Secondly, they own the natural resources, gold, banks, factories, land. Everything that in our system of political education is termed capitalism, stock market deals, exploitation, oppression, etc., etc.—all this is the province of rich Jews" (*ibid.*, p. 209).

become a political reality is most likely to come about given one of the following conditions: (a) the policy of Detente collapses once and for all, (b) total social stagnation leads to a massive cataclysm, or (c) the "mammoths" of the Politburo, who have barely thawed out from the ice age of Stalinism, simply die off.

I am not saying that this "right-wing" alternative would definitely become a political reality (there are other alternatives, which I have pointed out); I am simply saying that it *might* happen, and that the probability of its occurrence is great.

Chapter IV

CONCLUSIONS

1. It may seem strange to the reader that in a paper about Detente, I have devoted the first three chapters to sociopolitical portraits of different factions of the Soviet Establishment. But it seems exceedingly strange to me that after so many years of observation and study of the USSR, the strategy of Detente still somewhat resembles an old movie: it is hopelessly black-and-white. There is the "white" version: a bad peace is better than a good quarrel, so any contacts are better than nuclear war. Then there is the "black" version: by supplying the USSR with technology and credits, we are forgetting about Munich and helping to foster the rise of a new Hitler.

This sterile political dichotomy is a reflection of the black-and-white social model of the USSR that prevails—or that I think prevails—in the minds of millions of Americans: the two main social strata are the heroic dissident movement and the all-powerful Establishment, and the might of the latter is balanced by the saintly righteousness of the former.[1]

The key problem, from my standpoint, is that no such thing as an all-powerful Soviet Establishment exists. Moreover, there is no division of the Soviet Establishment into "hawks" and "doves," as the West likes to think. The society of the USSR is "multicolored," and the structure of the Soviet Establishment is complex and contradictory. Within it one can count at least five (or six) social groups unequally represented in the political leadership—groups whose interests are not only different, but sometimes opposed. No one of these groups is capable of exercising exclusive control over Soviet policy today. Therefore, the country is ruled by complex combinations of these groups: blocs or coalitions. While at present (let us assume) the situation is controlled by a right-center bloc, either a left-center bloc or a coalition of right-wing factions constitutes an

[1] I have already tried to call attention to the sterility of this model; see A. Yanov, "Detente and Soviet Managerial Class," *New York Times*, August 21, 1975.

alternative to it, as I have attempted to show. In other words, we are dealing at the very least with political algebra—not mere political arithmetic. From this "algebraic" standpoint, the working out of a constructive strategy of Detente by the West (not to speak of a *theory* of Detente, which not only does not exist, but which no one seems to have any intention of working out) requires above all that one find out what the objective interests and orientations of each of these blocs are. Then comes the time to decide which of these interests and orientations should be supported and which resisted, as well as how this is to be done.

The difference between the "black-and-white" and "multicolored" social models is by no means abstract, because different concrete political conclusions follow from each. Consider, for example, the manner in which the problem of American credits for the USSR is discussed on the basis of the black-and-white model. The proponents of the "white" view assert, in accord with the logic of their standpoint, that credits ought to be granted to the Soviet Establishment without any conditions. Their opponents, in accord with the logic of *their* standpoint, assert that credits should be preceded by the acceptance of a political ultimatum by the Soviet Establishment to ease the conditions for emigrating from the USSR and to liberalize the Soviet regime in general.

What might be the political consequences of these recommendations—from the standpoint of the "multicolor" model? It is clear that the "white" recommendation can only prolong the fruitless agony of the existing right-center bloc—with its inability to resist the claims of the military-industrial complex and, consequently, a new arms buildup; with its clumsy maneuvers aimed at combining Helsinki and Angola, which will mean new international crises; with its inability to solve the key problems of the country's economy, which will mean new economic and domestic political crises. Is this what the proponents of the "white" view want?

The "black" recommendation can produce one of two results: either the same result produced by the "white" recommendation, if the ultimatums are rejected; or, if they are accepted, stepped up activity by extreme reactionary forces, the triumph of the right-wing bloc and, ultimately, victory for the "right-wing" alternative.[2] Is this what the proponents of the "black" view want?

[2]It should be noted that the triumph of the "right-wing" alternative under the slogan "Steal what has been stolen!" (see ch. III, pp. 29ff.) would mean not only the end of Detente, but in all probability also a repudiation of all the debts of the antinational "old regime," as has already happened once in 1917. It is

From the standpoint of the "multicolor" model, the objective of Detente is neither trade with the USSR nor immediate political concessions, but rather to promote a course of events such that the USSR ceases to be a treacherous competitor undeserving of a single cent and becomes a business partner worthy of trust. Since this can come about only if the left-center bloc wins out in the domestic political struggle, the problem is not at all whether or not to give the USSR credits. The problem is *to whom* to give them and *for what.* Perhaps it will turn out that they should not be given at all to those who are now receiving and using them—i.e., the Ministry of Foreign Trade—but rather, for example, to the associations, the Soviet corporations. As indicated by certain signs (to which I have referred in my "portrait of a Soviet manager"), such an arrangement could be favorably received by certain segments of the Soviet leadership.[3] Moreover, this would not constitute a political ultimatum, but merely a business prerequisite for cooperation aimed at equalizing the status of the parties. It is perfectly natural for firms to deal with other firms, rather than with the state. From the political standpoint, this would mean a tremendous strengthening of the left-center orientation and, at the very least, a return to the 24th Congress (the congress of Detente) positions lost by Brezhnev. That is why study of the international structure of the Soviet Establishment and analysis of the interests of its various factions are a prerequisite for working out a sound and constructive strategy of Detente.

In essence the whole series of contradictory actions combining Detente and the arms race, "coexistence" and "ideological struggle," that we are used to calling Soviet policy is merely the visible surface, the perceptible result of a hidden and unstable balance of forces that take shape in various combinations as a consequence of conflicts and compromises among these factions. Why, for example, are there forty-five fully equipped divisions stationed at the Soviet-Chinese border—too many for protecting the border and too few for an invasion? You can look for a deep meaning in this absurdity for as long as you like if you proceed from the black-and-white model. But if you abandon that model, it becomes possible to construct, for instance, the following hypothesis: In 1969-70, after the armed suppression of the "Prague Spring" and the bloody incidents on the Chinese border, the Brezhnev faction lost control of the situation

quite clear that these debts would be treated as debts to the "Zionist-leaning" West—i.e., as money unjustly made by "world Jewry" from the sweat and blood of the working people (see ch. III, fn. 38).

[3] See pp. 37-38.

for a time, and the "invasion strategy" that prevailed at that time required a troop buildup on the border. When the Brezhnev faction, having successfully divided Shelepin and Polyansky and defeated them one at a time, regained control, it halted the buildup; but its power was not great enough to reduce these forces. What then had to happen if it did not want to build up these forces any further, but was unable to reduce them? An absurd situation had to ensue, and it has. The fabric of Soviet foreign policy is woven of such absurdities, contradictions, and actions undertaken but then stopped in the middle. From this standpoint, the key to Soviet foreign policy lies not so much in analyzing the various actions of the Soviet Establishment as in studying the disposition of social and political forces *within* this Establishment. From this standpoint, the endless debate about which motives dominate Soviet policy—ideological or pragmatic—loses its meaning. *Interests* dominate, and the complexity of the problem of interpreting Soviet policy lies in the fact that different interests dominate in different situations.

It follows that a knowledge of the internal structure of the Soviet Establishment must precede the elaboration of a constructive strategy of Detente. This requirement explains the structure of the present work: it is devoted to an analysis of the complex interrelationships among the interests that, depending on how they combine or conflict, will—in the author's opinion—determine the fate of Detente.

2. Now then, let us look at Detente from the standpoint of the interests of the strata described in the preceding chapters. We shall begin with the new "new class," for whom Detente ended the era of hypocritical Stalinist puritanism and initiated the era of genuine material abundance—"to each according to his needs," as promised in the *Communist Manifesto*. This new aristocracy no longer has any reason to bring about world revolution and build communism. It has already accomplished its revolution and built its communism. It needs only (a) *guarantees* of its prosperity, (b) *stabilization* of its aristocratic status, and (c) *legalization* of the hereditary nature of its privileges. To the aristocracy the West is not merely a technological El Dorado and source of credits without which it would no longer be possible to maintain the ailing Soviet economy;[4] the West is also

[4]If one is to believe the forecast made by the magazine *US News and World Report*, the Soviet economy, which is already growing more slowly than the American (4.5 percent per annum as compared to 6), will continue to grow more slowly to the end of the decade (4 percent as compared to 5.2 percent), thereby

an important source of its privileges.[5] If the monopoly on travel to the West held by this aristocracy is regarded by it as a privilege, then what sort of Detente can it desire? Can it want the sort of Detente demanded by Nobel Peace Prize winner Sakharov and the heroic Soviet dissidents: "opening up" the country completely and granting everyone the right to leave the country and return? That would deprive the aristocracy of one of its greatest privileges, which—strictly speaking—make it what it is today. That would mean suicide for the aristocracy as a social group. No, it does not want that kind of Detente.

On the other hand, does it want a restoration of Stalinism—with a new iron curtain and total terror, with an extreme narrowing of contacts with the West and a maximization of controls, with almost complete "closure" of the system and official puritanism that would eliminate the very possibility of legalization of its privileges? That also would mean suicide for the aristocracy.

What is left, then, if it does not want to "open up" or to "close" the system? What strategy could it choose—given its present understanding of the situation—to multiply and consolidate its privileges, rather than destroying itself? The one that it has already chosen—the strategy of "half-open doors." That is the strategy of Detente desired by the aristocracy, and the only one that is to its advantage today.

Of course, if pressed by the West, the aristocracy will make concessions, but only up to the point beyond which the process of self-destruction might begin. This means that it is of paramount importance for the West to understand exactly where that point is. This is where the problem becomes truly complex. On the one hand, the value of the Soviet aristocratic stratum from the standpoint of Detente is that it *can* be bargained with; in contrast to the hard-line, homogeneous Stalinist elite, it is prepared to consider the *extent* of concessions. But it is essential to understand that this stratum is subject to pressure from two sides—both from those who advocate

increasingly widening the gap between the two. One must not underestimate the social-psychological significance of this lag factor: it follows that the Soviet people not only will not live under communism by 1980, as promised in the CPSU Program, but they will *never* live under communism. Anyone who knows the psychology of the Soviet people will understand that the effect of exploding this myth will be much stronger than the effect of Khrushchev's revealing speech at the 20th Congress. If a further drop in the growth rate or economic stagnation is allowed to occur, the aristocracy may be swept away by a massive cataclysm.

[5] See ch. I, pp. 3-5.

"opening up" the system (the dissident movement supported by the West or, what is the same thing, the West supported by the dissident movement) and from those who advocate "closing" the system (the aristocracy's own partners in the right-center bloc).

Consequently, we must recognize that until the Soviet aristocracy overpowers its right-wing partners, until it has its privileges sanctioned and guaranteed, until it is institutionalized (not only de facto, but also de jure), the point of its self-destruction is dangerously close and the possibility of concessions on its part is minimized. In other words, the problem of "opening up" the system (or, in more general terms, the problem of successful Detente with the USSR) turns out to be directly dependent on the degree of aristocratization of the Soviet elite—dependent in a manner that, it may be said, can be measured with mathematical precision.

This pattern should be clear to anyone familiar with Russian history. Russia was also a "semi-open" country under Aleksey Mikhaylovich and became an "open" country under Catherine. Why? Because a new aristocracy became firmly established and no longer feared for its privileges. Why then could not a similar evolution take place in Soviet Russia? Has it ceased to be Russia?

The question arises of how and under what conditions the Soviet aristocracy could be institutionalized. In other words, under what conditions might the evolution of the system from semi-openness to openness be brought about? In the history of Russia there was another instance of, so to speak, an "abrupt" transition to an open system—i.e., when the Stalinist regime of Nicholas I, after a crushing military defeat, gave way to an era of liberal reforms. Under Alexander II, Russia was rapidly being liberalized and seemed already to have joined the European family of nations. At that time the foundations of power of the old slave-owning elite of Nicholas's reign were also undermined by a 20th Congress—that is to say, by the abolition of serfdom (which in principle may be equated to the dismantling of the Great GULAG)—and a new aristocracy (like that of today) was being born. In both cases the country's constructive development hinged on the same factor—on the institutionalization of a new hereditary Establishment, on the transformation of the elite into an aristocracy. Perhaps if at that time the West had mobilized its prodigious intellectual potential in order to promote this fundamental process (or had at least acknowledged its promotion to be one of its political aims), then there would have been no First World War, Russia would not have experienced another of its mindless autocratic explosions in 1917, and the West would not be confronted today by a mortal threat that causes trouble all over the world. The West did not act then, but why not learn from that mistake now at least—a tragic century later?

The task is one of tremendous—one may say historic—complexity. However, it is essentially similar to the one that confronted the "brain trust" on MacArthur's staff at the end of the Second World War. The difference is that at that time the Western intellectual community was able to *impose* a mode of liberalization on Japan, with its traditionally autocratic culture. Now it must develop an incomparably more delicate set of instruments for *convincing* one of the factions in an autocratic state to adopt the only possible strategy for its political survival—under conditions of peace and competition between ideas.

Because of the enormous complexity of this task, there are no easy solutions. It is impossible, for example, simply to "put pressure" on the Soviet Establishment because, as we have noted, it is still *becoming* an aristocracy: it has not completed the process yet. The aristocratic tendencies within the elite are so fragile and unstable that any excessive pressure might easily crush and destroy them, thereby depriving the West of a powerful potential ally within the Soviet Establishment.

But it would be an equal mistake to leave the Establishment to its own fate.[6] We have already seen that the Soviet aristocracy is not capable of controlling the situation by itself, that because of this it is now on the defensive rather than taking the offensive, and that its position is in jeopardy. As it begins to become clear that advanced Western technology—given the existing structure of the Soviet economy—is not functional, that the attempt to revive the corpse by means of injections of an alien substance is doomed, the aristocracy's position will be more and more jeopardized. The Soviets' own stock of ideas has already been exhausted—by Khrushchev's unsuccessful maneuvers, Kosygin's abortive reform, and Brezhnev's ineffectual "course"; therefore, ideological and intellectual "pressure" from the West is needed. Once again the question is not whether or not to "exert pressure," but *how much* pressure to exert and *where to direct it*. It is a question of ensuring that the pressure is skillfully applied, precisely calculated, constructive and—most important—goal-oriented. In other words, it is a matter of seeing to it that the the strategy and structure of Detente are appropriate to the internal political structure of the Soviet Establishment.

[6]See ch. I, pp. 16-21.

3. We have already said that if the aristocracy were to succeed in, so to speak, changing horses in midstream (breaking its traditional political alliance with the little Stalins and establishing a left-center coalition with the managers), there would be a second industrial revolution in Russia.[7] One of the social consequences of this revolution probably would be sharp differences among the working class. One has only to talk frankly with the directors of enterprises, state farms, and scientific institutes in order to be convinced that in their eyes the primary, insurmountable obstacle to production efficiency is the excess of manpower at their enterprises—what I call the "welfare economy." There is welfare in the West also, but it is separate from production. In Russia welfare has become an integral part of production; therefore, the idea of "separating welfare from production" dominates managers' thinking. The first thing they would do if they had free rein would be to discharge 40-50 percent of the workers and office employees.[8] The "separation of welfare from production" is the basis of the reasoning behind the Shchekino experiment, and it inspired the "autonomous link" movement in agriculture (the Pervitsky and Khudenko experiments),[9] the movement favoring brigade economic accountability in the construction industry (the Zlobin experiment), and a great many other less well-known experiments aimed at economic revitalization that are taking place in the Soviet economy today. The essence of these experiments is that groups of highly skilled workers, headed by a competent manager, are striving to get rid of the hordes of "welfare" parasites, which would enable them to set up a more rational production structure. The economic gain produced by these "guerilla operations" is indisputable. But what is to be done about their negative social effect? What is to be done with the tens of millions of workers who may be the victims of this revolution—i.e., who may be thrown out into the street, since the present Soviet economy is incapable of creating tens of millions of new jobs? Many Soviet managers are convinced that the prospect of massive unemployment was the reason for the collapse of Kosygin's reform and Brezhnev's "course"; it was, in any case, the principle argument used by their opponents—

[7] See ch. II, p. 29.

[8] That is the scale of the hidden unemployment in the Soviet economy (not 7-10 percent, as in the West) in the opinion of many managers.

[9] See my article "Behind Soviet Grain Purchases," *New York Times*, December 31, 1975.

the little Stalins—who assumed the role of "defenders of the proletariat."[10]

The ruling right-center bloc has demonstrated its inability to lead the urgently needed economic revolution. It allowed Khudenko to die in prison, permitted the Shchekino experiment to fizzle out, prevented the Zlobin experiment from expanding, and was unable to carry through either the reform of 1965 or the "course" of 1971. This is probably the primary reason for the steady decline experienced by the Soviet economy for almost two decades now. It is paradoxical that this decline can be explained very easily in Marxist terms: obsolete "production relations" are impeding the development of the "productive forces." That is the reason, according to Marx, for all the revolutions in history. Indeed, as I have attempted to show, the structure of the Soviet political organization is no longer in keeping with the complexity of the social system that it is attempting to govern. But no matter what the explanation is, one thing is clear: the aristocratic faction of the Soviet elite needs the assistance of the West in order to overcome economic stagnation. What form could this assistance take?

Everyone knows that the development of Siberia and the Far East has become a vital necessity for the USSR—both because of the exhaustion of resources in its western regions and because of the Chinese claims to these vast, half-empty expanses, which surpass Europe in area and wealth of natural resources.

The development of the American West was a powerful engine of rational economic development in the U.S. For many historical reasons, Russia has been unable to develop its "West" by itself. This is, if you will, the symbol and true measure of its historical backwardness. But this situation offers a unique opportunity for rationalizing Russia's further economic and social development. In this sense the development of the Far East could initiate the renaissance of a new Russia. Of course this can happen only if the development is not carried out by GULAG methods, as under Stalin, or by bureaucratically controlled methods, as under Brezhnev—only if it becomes a truly popular movement of reconstruction leading to a genuine economic revolution. But without advanced Western technology, without Western capital, without Western engineering, organizational, financial, and scientific "know-how," real development of the Russian East within the foreseeable future is inconceivable. What

[10]This argument is so widely known that it has even reached the cinema; see, for example, the film *Tvoy sovremenik* [Your contemporary].

is needed is a new Marshall Plan, if you will. It is necessary to mobilize the intellectual, technical, and financial resources of all the industrially developed countries and unite them with all the healthy and active elements in Russia. Why not return to Lenin's plan of developing the East on a joint concession basis, which was part of the old NEP? Why not offer Russia a new NEP over the huge expanses of Siberia? Why not help the historically positive faction of the Soviet Establishment to create millions of new jobs in the East, thereby eliminating the social hindrances to an industrial revolution in the Soviet West and simultaneously undermining the social foundation for the little Stalins? Why not make the construction of this new NEP an element of the strategy of Detente—provided of course that Detente is understood as promoting the transformation of the economic, social, and ultimately the political structure of the Russian autocracy?

Is it conceivable that autocratic Japan could have been transformed from a menacing potential enemy into a friendly business partner without a fundamental reorganization of its internal structure? The very same principle applies to Russia, for as long as it is an autocracy it will remain a threat to peace. It follows that if the overall objective of Detente is the establishment of a lasting peace, then the aims of Detente cannot be accomplished without transforming Russia.

How such a grandiose plan for developing the Soviet East could be worked out in the U.S. is not for me to judge: that requires a new Baruch or a new Marshall. But I have no reason to think that a nation that was able to raise Europe from ruins might shrink from the problem of devising such a plan. All I can say here is that such a constructive and creative interpretation of Detente—so far as I can judge—would be welcomed in the USSR both by the centrist groups in the Soviet leadership and by the majority of the managerial class, for whom it would open the way to becoming part of the leadership.

4. It remains for us to discuss how Detente relates to the realm of ideas. We have already discussed the new "masters of the minds" of thinking young Russians—Dostoyevsky and Berdyayev.[11] In the

[11] See ch. III, p. 68. I would like my views to be understood properly. I have the greatest respect both for Dostoyevsky's artistic genius and Berdyayev's philosophical views and for the heroism of their mighty follower Solzhenitsyn. What seems dangerous to me is the tendency toward national messianism in their creative works—the conviction that Russia is a "special civilization" historically

fermenting vat of ideas that I consider Russia to be today, in the explosive atmosphere in which it must mature, the national-messianic orientation of these teachers, which is derived from the postulate that there is no hope for the "rotting" West, may prove to be a menace of the first order. Essentially it is capable of ruining the attempt at reconstruction, even if objective conditions favorable to it arise. There is no doubt that the right-wing bloc, if it loses its parliamentary majority (and with it the chance to prevent the reconstruction by legal means), will resort to nonparliamentary means, to the nationalistically minded youth, who will take to "the streets."[12] The response to stepped up activity by "right-wing" extremists will be, as has always been the case in Russia, stepped up activity by "left-wing" extremists. The result may be a new cataclysm that could end in a victory for the isolationist "right-wing" alternative. That is why the strategy of Detente cannot fail to take this into account, and why fostering the development of a positive climate of ideas in Russia should be an integral part of that strategy.

Of course I do not mean to imply that the Western intellectual community should take the place of the Russian intellectual community in accomplishing pressing tasks in the realm of ideas—above all, the necessary revision of Marxism. Western assistance is needed only with regard to what Russian thought cannot do by itself at the present time because of the yoke of censorship. I have in mind mainly two things. The first is to do battle against the conceptual foundation of the "right-wing" alternative: the national-messianic ideology. It should not be forgotten that whereas during the sixty years of its domination, Marxist "internationalism" has managed to demonstrate categorically its bankruptcy in the realm of ideas and its inability to bring about a national renaissance, nothing of the sort has occurred in the case of the "right-wing" alternative. Its Black Hundred, imperial-isolationist potentialities have not become historical facts and are therefore little known in Russia today. The inability of the "right-wing" alternative to solve the nation's problems has not been demonstrated in practice. It is remembered as a beautiful legend, as an unrealized opportunity for national renaissance that perished in the struggle against anti-national Bolshevism.

destined to bring "new light" to the world, and the urge to represent the traditional backwardness of Russian political culture as the acme and crowning glory of human thought.

[12] For example, it would be fairly easy to portray the joint reconstruction of the Soviet East as the expansion of "Jewish" capital, as a new attempt by "Jewish" capital to make Russia its colony.

Therefore the popularity of the emigre Berdyayev, who preached socialism (but without the communists) along with the sacred truth of the "Russian idea," is only natural. The young and inexperienced national consciousness that is rising again "from under the rubble" is seeking a historical platform for itself, and it is finding a thoroughly elaborated system of ideas that predicted even before 1917 that a Marxist experiment would be disastrous for Russia. If history has confirmed the correctness of Berdyayev's negative prophecies—so goes the argument—then it is reasonable to assume that his positive recommendations are also correct. "Young Russia" believes in them, wants to believe in them. Soviet Marxist thought is no match for Berdyayev; its influence is insignificant, it has been compromised, and on top of everything else it is bound hand and foot by dogmas and censorship. As experience has shown, the liberal Samizdat is also not strong enough to contend against national messianism.[13]

It is here that the help of the Western intellectual community is as important as the help of Western capital in the reconstruction of the Soviet East. But here we encounter a surprising phenomenon: the ideology of the "right-wing" alternative is as little known in the West as it is in Russia. A great many books have been written about the Bolsheviks, the Mensheviks, the Socialist Revolutionaries, and the Cadets, but try to name even one book about the Russian "right"—about Sharapov, the "League of the Russian People," the even more radical "League of Michael the Archangel," the Black Hundred movement in the Duma and in the streets, about Stalin as the heir of Purishkevich. In other words, try to name a book about the objective patterns in the evolution of the "Russian idea" from the nobel striving to "liberate the national soul" to national-socialism. The "Russian idea" has never stood "before the bar of history." I can think of no more fruitful task for Sovietologists than to put this idea on trial before history, for that is the only thing, if we are to believe the venerable Freud, that can break the hold of the fatal national inferiority complex over the minds of valiant Russian youth, thereby undermining the ideological foundation for the little Stalins. For the Western intellectual community to be involved in the accomplishment of this task would mean being involved in a genuinely creative

[13]See, for example, the polemic that followed V. Gorsky's article "Russian Messianism and the New National Consciousness" in the journal *Vestnik russkogo studencheskogo khristianskogo dvizheniya*, No. 97, 1970. This demonstrates what a storm of indignation was provoked among nationalistic young people by a proposal to disavow the idea of messianism. See also A. Solzhenitsyn's article "Obrazovanshchina" [The smatterers] in the collection *Iz-pod glyb* [From under the rubble].

historical act. It would mean that along with politicians, economists, engineers, and managers, there is a place in the strategy of Detente for historians, sociologists, philosophers, and "political scientists"—particularly because this does not exhaust the tasks posed by Detente in the realm of ideas. It is only the beginning, if one recalls the furious and fruitless struggle between the Russian aristocracy and the Russian intellectual community,[14] between the traditional egalitarian and moral maximalism of the intelligentsia, which rejects privileges in principle, and the haughty intolerance of the intellectually and ethically detrimental new "new class." Serving as an arbiter between these two groups, finding common ground on which these current enemies and potential allies could come together for positive and creative statecraft, in any case demonstrating to both sides the organic connection between sanctioning privileges and preventing a restoration of Stalinism—these are things that no one but the Western intellectual community would be able to do.

5. Everybody in Russia today knows that things are going badly, but no one knows what to do to make them go well. And what about the U.S.? Isn't the same thing true of the U.S.?[15] Why is the temper of two countries with such different, even opposite social systems so similar? I think it is because the reason is the same: only a great aim gives rise to great energy. Where is this aim?

Such an aim could be the establishment of a firm and lasting peace on earth, a peace that would provide an opportunity to give intensive thought to the urgent global problems that threaten the very existence of mankind—the world food crisis, the population explosion, the exhaustion of the earth's resources, the poisoning of the environment—and perfecting the political mechanisms that will make it possible to concentrate mankind's enormous intellectual powers on solving these problems. How is such a peace to be achieved? What paths lead to it?

I say that Detente leads to this kind of peace if Detente is understood not as a matter of momentary interests, not as trade as an end in itself, and not as trifling concessions by authoritarian regimes, but as a gigantic battle of ideas—the first attempt in his-

[14]See ch. I, pp. 15-16.

[15]A friend of mine wrote recently from Moscow: "How do you explain the fact that American 'eggheads,' who arranged the destiny of Japan with such wisdom and are able to predict human destiny a quarter of a century in advance, have gotten lost so suddenly in their own extremely comfortable world?"

tory, in peacetime and using peaceful means, to utilize the intellectual might of "political civilization" to transform "political barbarism."

Yes, Detente is an alternative not only to the fear of global war, not only to the ruinous arms race whose end is not in sight, but also to the erosion of democracy. Democracy today is an island in a raging sea of authoritarianism, a fortress under siege. It is compelled to be militarized in a militarized world; the task of survival takes precedence over the task of solving the most complex problems of its internal development. But dynamic systems cannot mark time: they either develop or degenerate. The student disturbances of the 1960's, the Watergate scandal, and the authoritarian actions of the FBI are ominous signs of degeneration. They are natural in the environment of a besieged fortress: war is war. Militarism, extremism, and degeneration can be countered only by a great, peaceful, ideological and intellectual offensive against authoritarianism—in both domestic and foreign policy. The apathy and disillusionment of the young can be countered only by mobilizing all the spiritual energy of the free world, as well as of all the historically positive elements within the authoritarian systems.

Commenting on Dr. Kissinger's favorite argument—peace is the only alternative to nuclear war—a linguist would say that it is a tautology. A philosopher must say more, for this tautology not only indicates the strategic futility of this transitional period in world politics, but also offers an accurate reflection of this period when war is no longer functional as a means of resolving global conflicts, but peace has not yet been acknowledged as such a means. As the experience of the Paris agreements on Vietnam shows, the peace can be lost—just as wars are lost. Does it not follow that the peace can also be won?

INSTITUTE OF INTERNATIONAL STUDIES
UNIVERSITY OF CALIFORNIA, BERKELEY

CARL G. ROSBERG,
Director

Monographs published by the Institute include:

RESEARCH SERIES

1. *The Chinese Anarchist Movement*, by Robert A. Scalapino and George T. Yu ($1.00)
3. *Land Tenure and Taxation in Nepal*, Volume I, *The State as Landlord: Raikar Tenure*, by Mahesh C. Regmi. ($8.75; unbound photocopy)
4. *Land Tenure and Taxation in Nepal*, Volume II, *The Land Grant System: Birta Tenure*, by Mahesh C. Regmi. ($2.50)
6. *Local Taxation in Tanganyika*, by Eugene C. Lee. ($1.00)
7. *Birth Rates in Latin America: New Estimates of Historical Trends*, by O. Andrew Collver. ($2.50)
8. *Land Tenure and Taxation in Nepal*, Volume III, *The Jagir, Rakam, and Kipat Tenure Systems*, by Mahesh C. Regmi ($2.50)
9. *Ecology and Economic Development in Tropical Africa*, edited by David Brokensha. ($8.25; unbound photocopy)
12. *Land Tenure and Taxation in Nepal*, Volume IV, *Religious and Charitable Land Endowments: Guthi Tenure*, by Mahesh C. Regmi ($2.75)
13. *The Pink Yo-Yo: Occupational Mobility in Belgrade, ca 1915-1965*, by Eugene A. Hammel. ($2.00)
14. *Community Development in Israel and the Netherlands: A Comparative Analysis*, by Ralph M. Kramer. ($2.50)
*15. *Central American Economic Integration: The Politics of Unequal Benefits*, by Stuart I. Fagan. ($2.00)
16. *The International Imperatives of Technology: Technological Development and the International Political System*, by Eugene B. Skolnikoff. ($2.95)
*17. *Autonomy or Dependence as Regional Integration Outcomes: Central America*, by Philippe C. Schmitter. ($1.75)
18. *Framework for a General Theory of Cognition and Choice*, by R.M. Axelrod. ($1.50)
19. *Entry of New Competitors in Yugoslav Market Socialism*, by S.R. Sacks. ($2.50)
*20. *Political Integration in French Speaking Africa*, by Abdul A. Jalloh. ($3.50)
21. *The Desert and the Sown: Nomads in the Wider Society*, ed. by Cynthia Nelson. ($3.50)
22. *U.S.-Japanese Competition in International Markets: A Study of the Trade-Investment Cycle in Modern Capitalism*, by John E. Roemer. ($3.95)
23. *Political Disaffection Among British University Students: Concepts, Measurement, and Causes*, by Jack Citrin and David J. Elkins. ($2.00)
24. *Urban Inequality and Housing Policy in Tanzania: The Problem of Squatting*, by Richard E. Stren. ($2.50)
*25. *The Obsolescence of Regional Integration Theory*, by Ernst B. Haas. ($2.95)
26. *The Voluntary Service Agency in Israel*, by Ralph M. Kramer. ($2.00)
27. *The SOCSIM Demographic-Sociological Microsimulation Program: Operating Manual*, by Eugene A. Hammel *et al.* ($4.50)
28. *Authoritarian Politics in Communist Europe: Uniformity & Diversity in One-Party States*, edited by Andrew C. Janos. ($3.75)

*International Integration Series

INSTITUTE OF INTERNATIONAL STUDIES MONOGRAPHS (*continued*)

29. *The Anglo-Icelandic Cod War of 1972-1973: A Case Study of a Fishery Dispute*, by Jeffrey A. Hart. ($2.00)
30. *Plural Societies and New States: A Conceptual Analysis*, by Robert Jackson. ($2.00)
31. *The Politics of Crude Oil Pricing in the Middle East, 1970-1975: A Study in International Bargaining*, by Richard Chadbourn Weisberg. ($3.50)
32. *Agricultural Policy and Performance in Zambia: History, Prospects, and Proposals for Change*, by Doris Jansen Dodge. ($4.95)
33. *Five Classy Programs: Computer Procedures for the Classification of Households*, by E.A. Hammel and R.Z. Deuel. ($3.75)
34. *Housing the Urban Poor in Africa: Policy, Politics, and Bureaucracy in Mombasa*, by Richard E. Stren ($5.95)
35. *The Russian New Right: Right-Wing Ideologies in the Contemporary USSR*, by Alexander Yanov. ($3.95)
36. *Social Change in Romania, 1860-1940: A Debate on Development in a European Nation*, ed. by Kenneth Jowitt. ($4.50)

POLITICS OF MODERNIZATION SERIES

1. *Spanish Bureaucratic-Patrimonialism in America*, by Magali Sarfatti ($2.00)
2. *Civil-Military Relations in Argentina, Chile, and Peru*, by Liisa North. ($2.00)
3. *Notes on the Process of Industrialization in Argentina, Chile, and Peru*, by Alcira Leiserson. ($1.75)
4. *Chilean Christian Democracy: Politics and Social Forces*, by James Petras ($1.50)
5. *Social Stratification in Peru*, by Magali S. Larson and Arlene E. Bergman. ($4.95)
6. *Modernization and Coercion*, by Mario Barrera. ($1.50)
7. *Latin America: The Hegemonic Crisis and the Military Coup*, by José Nun. ($2.00)
8. *Development Processes in Chilean Local Government*, by Peter S. Cleaves. ($1.50)
9. *Modernization and Bureaucratic-Authoritarianism: Studies in South American Politics*, by Guillermo A. O'Donnell. ($3.50)

POLICY PAPERS IN INTERNATIONAL AFFAIRS

1. *Images of Detente and the Soviet Political Order*, by Kenneth Jowitt. ($1.00)
2. *Detente After Brezhnev: The Domestic Roots of Soviet Foreign Policy*, by Alexander Yanov. ($3.00)
3. *The Mature Neighbor Policy: A New United States Economic Policy for Latin America*, by Albert Fishlow. ($2.00)
4. *Five Images of the Soviet Future: A Critical Review and Synthesis*, by George W. Breslauer. ($2.50)
5. *Global Evangelism Rides Again: How to Protect Human Rights Without Really Trying*, by Ernst B. Haas. ($2.00)
6. *Israel and Jordan: The Implications of an Adversarial Partnership*, by Ian Lustick. ($2.00)
7. *Political Syncretism in Italy: Historical Coalition Strategies and the Present Crisis*, by Giuseppe Di Palma. ($2.00)

Address correspondence to:

Institute of International Studies
215 Moses Hall
University of California
Berkeley, California 94720